SMALL CHANGE

A History of
Everyday Coinage

Peter Johnson

AMBERLEY

For Bunty the Barber (Arthur Woodhead of Eckington), who encouraged a young lad's numismatic interests, and my mother, for patiently nurturing the development of said interests.

First published 2019

Amberley Publishing
The Hill, Stroud
Gloucestershire, GL5 4EP

www.amberley-books.com

British Library Cataloguing in Publication Data.
A catalogue record for this book is available from the British Library.

ISBN 978 1 4456 8970 8 (print)
ISBN 978 1 4456 8971 5 (ebook)

Typeset in 9.5pt on 12.5pt Sabon.
Origination by Amberley Publishing.
Printed in the UK.

Introduction

'A plentiful and convenient copper coinage seems to us of the present day to be an obvious necessity, but as a matter of fact the country suffered for centuries for the want of small money.' This claim was made by David Murray during a talk presented to Glasgow Archaeological Society on 16 February 1882. He was talking not just of Scotland, but about all the nations of the United Kingdom. In *Small Change: A History of Everyday Coinage*, centrally issued denominations – on the occasions they were produced – are examined within their historical context. Equal emphasis is given to those fascinating unofficial and local responses to government inactivity.

The first part introduces aspects of everyday coinage within a worldwide context; these reappear in the second part which traces the British experience of small change through the centuries. In some sections the coins and tokens illustrate themes arising in the main text, in others the coins speak for themselves through extended captions after a short introduction. Their size is indicated by the range of diameters given in the caption for those shown.

In late Anglo-Saxon times British currency was based on the penny. Gradually, as history unfolded, bringing with it changing conditions and novel opportunities, new denominations came into being and by the early modern period the principal elements of the currency became pounds, shillings and pence. In shorthand these were written as L.S.D. (or £.s.d.). Older readers might remember prices given as £4/16/11, sometimes £4 16s 11d (four pounds, sixteen shillings and eleven pence), and other strange-looking expressions. This notation was based on Latin: Librae (libra – a pound weight), Solidii (solidus – a gold coin), Denarii (denarius – a silver coin). There were twelve pennies to every shilling (now 5p), and twenty shillings, or 240 pennies, to a pound. Fractions or multiples of these, such as halfpennies, sixpences and half-crowns (two-and-half shillings), were also issued. It all made sense at the time.

Peter Johnson
March 2019

Part One

The World of Small Change

A World Without Coins

Set against the many millennia that humans have roamed the earth, coinage is a recent invention. For the greater part of human existence hunter-gatherers and subsequent settled communities were self-sufficient. When they were short of a resource they bartered for what they needed in exchange for items they had a surplus of, or took on relative values of account between different specialists – a bronze axe might have equalled two small coracles, both of which were worth four roof timbers. Reciprocal gift exchanges of precious, scarce or high-status items between leaders of groups were a further method of ensuring that economies and their underlying social structures ran reasonably smoothly. Trade and exchange links could cover wide areas. Axes derived from the plentiful ores of the Bronze Age copper mines on the Great Orme, Llandudno, have been located in northern mainland Europe. Indeed, great civilisations in past times have managed to conduct their affairs quite satisfactorily, often over extensive territories, without a brass farthing between them – the ancient Egyptians, Hittites, Incas and the kingdom of Benin to name but a few. Of course, wars, raids and plunder were further means of gaining resources, both animate and inanimate.

The citadel of Mycenae offers insights into the workings of a pre-coin society. Between 1400 and 1100 BC it dominated the southern parts of Greece and the Aegean and left behind in the archaeological record a large number of clay tablets inscribed with hieroglyphics. This script, Linear B, was discovered to be an early form of Greek. The tablets tell of complex systems for social organisation, bureaucratic methods, agriculture, land ownership and industry and trade. The society was headed by a king, probably a priest-king, who ran an efficient civil service, below which lay a hierarchy of farmers and tradespeople. Allowing for local variations in regions of the realm, much of the produce these people created was controlled by the palace and redistributed accordingly. Although money was not a part of these activities, the concepts of exchange, equivalent values and order had been established, as it had been in all the great ancient societies.

For many of these civilisations precious metals, especially gold, or forged bars of utilitarian iron or copper were traded by weight. In Egypt and Mesopotamia these pieces were firmly standardised and regulated by the king or temple. Yet these artefacts were not coins. The Lydian Greeks of what is now western Turkey had access to a plentiful supply of electrum – a naturally occurring mixture of gold and silver – from the

Bronze palstave axe manufactured near Llandudno, *c.* 1500–1400 BC, a type which directly or via a series of exchanges journeyed to mainland Europe. Electrum twelfth-stater with the head of roaring lion, radiate nodule on forehead, and an incuse square, from the Lydian Kingdom of Alyattes or Croesus (*c.* 610–546 BC). (*c.* 160 mm, 7 mm. Not to scale.) (Courtesy of Great Orme Mines and wildwinds.com)

River Pactolus which ran through their territory. They valued these nuggets by weight in the traditional manner. At some time in the seventh century BC the idea was borne of producing small lumps of equal weight and stamping them with a consistent design to confirm their value and authenticity. Very soon the Lydians were fabricating these in a range of carefully controlled weights. The idea and practice quickly spread around the eastern Mediterranean: coinage had arrived in the western world.

Non-Coin Small Change: Shells

Many objects and materials have served for the purpose of exchange or valuing a person's worth for various groups around the world, as befitted their culture and availability of resources. These non-coin currencies have included items as diverse as unworked metal, large stones, tobacco, salt, rice, cattle, silk, cloth and shells.

Someone we know has just bought something, and we ask, informally, 'How much did you have to shell out on that then?' If they answered, quite honestly, 'Ten cowries', we might be a little perplexed. The phrase 'shell out', meaning 'to pay' or 'paid', was probably first used around AD 1800, a figurative expression based on removing peas from a pod – taking money from a purse. Using actual shells for transactions has been recorded from regions in Asia, Africa, North America and Australia for many peoples who were essentially self-sufficient.

The tropical sea-dwelling money cowrie (*Monetaria moneta*) has a translucent and attractive shell about 1–2.5 cm long, which is quite robust. These offer the earliest known examples of 'shells-as-money', appearing in China around 1500 BC – and 'ten cowries' then could have been a quite legitimate answer. Centuries later these shells continued to be a medium of exchange in many Pacific and Indian Ocean countries and vast quantities were harvested from the Maldives. A great number were taken into West Africa by slave traders, with them being more valued the further inland they were taken. The shell of the ring-top cowrie (*Monetaria annulus*) is another species exploited in tropical lands and was introduced to Native Americans by European fur traders as a

Just over fifty cowrie shells (*Monetaria annulus*). The smallest denomination issued in Bengal in 1780 was one-sixteenth anna, shown here. One rupee was worth sixteen annas; therefore, there were 256 one-sixteenths of an anna to every rupee. The twelve money cowries (*Monetaria moneta*) were worth about one-sixteenth of an anna; thus the coin would have been impractical in circumstances where the purchase was for something costing, say, three or four cowries. This little pile also suggests that the heap of *Monetaria annulus* could have been worth a relatively significant amount. For an unknown reason someone had attempted to drill a hole through the chunky copper coin from pre-twentieth century northern India and in doing so had accidently split it into two pieces. Rather than lose what must have been its limited purchasing power it was repaired with thin wire – a quite touching illustration of the value of small change for those who may not have had very much. (Cowries *c.* 20 mm–22 mm, coins 19 mm–20 mm.)

Painting from 1845 depicting an Arab trader with his open bag of cowrie shells.

cheaper substitute for highly treasured, but much scarcer, elk ivory. The last shells to be commonly employed for transactional purposes were from the crescent-shaped *kina*, which remained operative in Papua New Guinea into the twentieth century.

The use of cowries for small transactions was particularly prevalent in areas of India up to the nineteenth century, particularly Bengal, north-eastern India. In this region the British-controlled East India Company gradually increased its influence after first arriving in the late seventeenth century. In 1757, rather than pay those employed building the fortifications of Fort William, Calcutta, in the local currency of cowrie shells, they issued (now rare) base metal monetary tickets. Some decades later, in 1780, the company contracted prominent Calcutta merchant James Prinsep to supply a copper coinage bearing local inscriptions to standardise the basis of transactions, and offered an exchange rate of one rupee for every 5,120 cowries. This endeavour failed as the new money could not rival the cowrie. As well as familiarity in using shells and fundamentally knowing their value, perhaps they also enabled buyers to purchase extremely low cost items for which no sufficiently small denomination coins had been minted. By 1795 new copper coins had been struck and gradually the cowrie faded from the marketplace as this coinage and European ways of working were brought into the economy.

Other than by invasion and imposition, the transition from ancient ways and non-coin currencies to economies based on coined money was likely to have been a gradual process for most. For some folk this period could have been quite fraught as no doubt chancers and other miscreants (at all levels of society) took the opportunity to make something of an 'extravagant' profit. Perhaps certain factors arising from changes in currency over the last fifty years or so – decimalisation, the introduction of the Euro – have historical precedents.

What is 'Small Change'?

'Small change' is a slippery concept, as defining its upper limit – 1p? 50p? £1? £10? – depends on one's income and expenditure. When historical dimensions and worldwide variations between rich and poor are added to this, then defining 'small change' becomes yet more challenging.

A number of attempts have been made over the years to convert historical costs and incomes into present-day values, but with variable success. One difficulty is that resources can be common or scarce over the years: bread is cheap when harvests are good and expensive – perhaps prohibitively so – when they fail. Additionally, the availability of a workforce can alter basic costs as incomes rise and fall according to whether there is a shortage or surplus of workers in any particular period. Inflation, boom and bust economics, national crises, and changes in the value of bullion (the raw material for coin manufacture) are among other factors which can distort the picture.

There is another complication. Presently, in 2019, the smallest denomination British coin is the 1p; yet by itself this does not describe the full range of realistic values for 'small change'. In other times and places the smallest denominations were made of silver (or even gold), without any base metal issues, and would be far too high in value for buying, say, a loaf of bread from the corner shop. Allowing for these complications, and using as a very rough guide values in Britain in 2019, 'small change' will be understood as coins, or something used in their place, loosely equivalent to no more than £5. For other parts of the world and different historical periods, the lower denominations of money used

Large copper coins: Ptolemy IV, Hellenistic king of Egypt (221–204 BC), four obols; Carl XI, Sweden, 1673, one öre; Catherine II, Russia, 1789, five kopeks; George III, Great Britain, 1797, 'cartwheel' twopence. (42 mm, 71.9 g; 47 mm, 41.1g; 45 mm, 53.3 g; 40 mm, 57.7 g.)

Small 'change' from Greece and India. Silver: Uncertain mint in Ionia, head of Apollo, quartered incuse square, *c. 500 BC*; Athens, head of Athena, owl, 449–413 BC; Rhodes, radiate head of the sun god Helios, two rosebuds with a microscopic Artemis running between them holding a torch, 304–167 BC; Masikytes, a member of the Lycian League, bust of Artemis, quiver and palm branch in incuse square, first century BC. The celebrated Athenian playwright Aristophanes tells us in his 422 BC production *The Wasps* that the tiny coins of Athens were carried to market in their owners' mouths, though men had to beware being amorously kissed along the way and having them stolen. Incredibly, the smallest coin issued in fourth-century Athens was the hemitartemorion that weighed in at a miniscule 0.09 g. No wonder then that by 350 BC a token coinage of somewhat larger bronze coins had been introduced in their place. Two gold fanams of nearly identical weight feature from south-west India, *c. AD 1600–1900. (6 mm, 0.36 g; 7 mm 0.33 g; 9 mm, 0.91 g; 11 mm, 0.71 g; both *c. 8 mm and 0.38 g.)

Other forms of small change. China, Emperor Wang Mang, AD 9–23, bronze Pu currency in the shape of a spade. 'Pieces of Eight' (often associated with pirates) were eight reales pieces rendered from silver mined in Spanish territories in South America. The irregular lump of silver is a two reales bullion piece from Potosí, Bolivia, 1743. Emergency (or necessity) money – *Notgeld* – for five pfennigs issued as paper money in Elberfeld, Germany, March 1920. (58 mm; 22 mm; 59 mm by 43 mm.)

by those societies – insofar as they might be of value for purchasing lesser commodities (in price, though not necessarily in importance) – can be considered 'small change'.

The physical manifestation of everyday coinage nowadays is considered to be coins, usually round, occasionally square, or near equivalent geometric shapes, made in base metals such as bronze or cupro-nickel, with a diameter no greater than 30 mm. This generalisation has not always held true. There have been some quite hefty copper coins produced over the last 2,300 years, and many tiny ones in silver and gold. Furthermore, some small change has been fashioned in quite irregular or surprising shapes, and not all have been in metal.

Imitations, Counterfeits, Forgeries and Fakes

These terms can cause great confusion, perhaps because they are interchangeable in everyday speech for any copy of an object. For present purposes the term 'imitation' will be applied to a coin that copies another in some respect but does not aim to defraud or deceive. They can be produced to signal allegiances or to facilitate trade. The word 'counterfeit' can mean either a coin produced contemporary with an original so as to pass as legal tender, or a recent copy designed to swindle collectors and museums. As this is somewhat ambiguous, 'forgery' is the preferred term for unlawful copies of coins produced at the time the original was current. Forgeries may be almost indistinguishable from the real thing, even for an expert; they can also be rather rudimentary in their manufacture, as the coin from Spain demonstrates. These activities

700 years of small owls (and a tiny cicada). From its inception around 510 BC, large Athenian silver tetradrachms were known as 'owls' due to the portrayal of this bird, sacred to Athena, on the reverse. They were recognised as an international standard for weight and fineness throughout the eastern Mediterranean and were extensively imitated. This influence also found favour in the design of small change. The small silver coins, top left, are an Athenian trihemiobol and an obol, both from 449–413 BC, with helmeted head of Athena, owl and 'AΘE' – '(money) of the Athenians'. Presenting only the reverses, the third is from Kamarina, Sicily, an ally of Athens in her war on that island, dating from 413–405 BC. The next, from Sigeion, Troas, near the entrance to the Hellespont, dates *c.* 350 BC. The fifth, with two owls, from Athens, was minted in the third century BC, as was the silver hemidrachm from Amisus, Pontus, on the Black Sea coast. The larger bronze is again from Athens, 229–166 BC. The coin from Pergamon, Mysia, was issued during the second or first century BC while that from Laodicea ad Mare, on the Syrian coast, dates from the Roman period, first and second centuries AD. The final owl from Athens, from the third century AD, is 700 years later than the first and the symbolism remains virtually unchanged. The owl was not the only creature to appear on Athenian coinage; for example, the tiny coin showing a cicada dates from 220–83 BC, though this design was not imitated. (9 mm–21 mm.)

have been undertaken with rare and precious pieces: as circumstances dictated, small denomination coins have also been subject to them. 'Fakes' can be taken to be modern copies and concoctions. These have no place here and will not be considered further – with the one proviso of a hope that none will be found in any of the illustrations in these pages.

Small denomination Spanish copper coins were crudely struck up to the eighteenth century. The first is an official issue of sixteen maravedis from the mint of Segovia, 1662, for the proudly moustachioed Philip IV (1621–1665). The second is a contemporary forgery of this coin and its rudimentary execution has produced an almost comic effect. The obverse die was engraved as the official coin looked, producing a mirrored image on the blank, resulting in the king facing the wrong way and a corrupt legend. That such a low denomination coin should be forged might suggest either a largely depleted store of small change in circulation, or an exhausted supply of any change in a desperate person's pocket. (23 mm–25 mm.)

Adaptations

Over the ages small change has been adapted for purposes other than those originally intended. In the process it has suffered many indignities: for example, being engraved upon, used as instruments of damnation, cut into pieces, clipped and countermarked. All this activity might be considered as simply deforming the coin. Alternatively, it can be suggested that it makes for an inherently intriguing series: they are examples of currency in use with which users, as it were, interacted. Sometimes small change was adapted for quite unexpected reasons.

Untold thousands of countermarks (also called counterstamps) have been applied to coins, almost from the time they were first invented. They may be employed in very specific circumstances or play a far wider-ranging role than other adaptations. Countermarks are defined as a mark, usually a stamp, occasionally a set of single punches, impressed upon a coin or token. Though more commonly found on lower denominations, countermarks could be applied to gold (albeit rarely) and silver. On official productions they can guarantee its weight, legitimise it as legal tender (in some other currency, region or state), increase or decrease its value, produce an emergency currency, or render it obsolete and illegal. The information gained from these coins, often as unwitting testimony, can offer insights into local conditions.

The picture becomes a little murkier when countermarks on tokens and official issues used privately are considered. At a basic level the reason for the practice depends simply on two or more persons agreeing what is meant by it. These countermarks were applied in quite dissimilar circumstances: to manufacture a circulating medium when adequate official issues did not exist, to indicate a new owner of a premises, to produce an advertising medium, to circumvent laws prohibiting use of a particular token issue, to indicate the amount of real money owed for completing a task, and to act as a ticket (for example, picking up an item previously paid for). By the very nature of the subject this list is not exhaustive.

All this leads to the circumstance that the source of many countermarks and for what purpose they were produced cannot be identified. Specious and errant issues ('sports') –

Many smaller denomination coins and tokens can be found which have been punched or engraved with one or two names or initials, sometimes a date, and occasionally a slogan. The more extravagant examples may have a heart or other sign incised upon them; yet others may have been crafted to deliver a message held dear by the engraver. These one-offs are generally considered to be love tokens, perhaps given to emphasise affection or to be remembered after death, when sent away to war, or transported to penal colonies in Australia – 'forget-me-not'. It is most unlikely that we will ever know why Edwin Barringer engraved this worn coin with the slogan 'Keep Holy The Sabbath Day', dated 21 March 1840. Elizabeth Bird ('Born 19 August 1810') and William Maskell ('Dear Sister, May love and Friendship Never be forgot, 1818') engraved – by themselves or by a 'professional' hand – smoothed obverses of pennies from 1797. They were very likely to have been convicts transported to Australia. (c. 35 mm.) (The last two courtesy of Museums Victoria)

Damnatio (condemnation). History might portray a ruler as the doer of good works – majestic architecture, artwork, and innovations of diverse sorts carried out during that period of administration. For some (or all) of those who were ruled, however, said ruler might have been thoroughly despised, and what better way to wreak vengeance on a loathed monarch than violence by proxy: giving the ruler's effigy on coins 'a bit of a seeing to' which others will see when it cautiously re-enters circulation. The first example from Smyrna (now Izmir) was produced for the unstable Roman emperor Germanicus (known by his nickname Caligula), AD 37–41. He is credited with committing many foul acts during his reign, including having an incestuous relationship with his sister Drusilla, who is shown on the reverse of this coin. The *damnatio* here has been applied to Caligula's neck, as if symbolically decapitating him, by pressure from a hard implement. It was attacked at least four times, sufficiently strongly to warp the coin, though being produced by pressure rather than by impact no shadow appears on the reverse. The Austrian three kreuzer of Franz II from 1800 has been gouged to form a cross over his head. Three times he lost battles with Napoleon and had to concede territory; reinstituted much of the power of the Roman Catholic Church; dissolved the Holy Roman Empire in 1806 (ruling until 1835 as Franz I of Austria); and had an extensive and very active network of police spies and censors. How could he have been unpopular with someone? (18 mm, 28 mm.)

During periods when the smallest denomination available of thin hammered coin was higher than the cost of many purchases, smaller change could be fashioned by the simple employment of a pair of shears. A penny from late in the reign of King John (1199–1216) – around the time he signed Magna Carta at Runnymede – has been cut in half to make this halfpenny. Other variations, such as a fourth-thing (farthing), were also rendered in this manner. The short cross on the reverse made an excellent guide for this process, especially for those officially cut at the mint. That the example here has been cut obliquely suggests that the shears were deployed by a private citizen. The complete penny of John from around 1205 was struck under royal licence by Rauf at the mint in London. Small change could be made even smaller, dishonestly. The maltreated short-cross penny could be an issue of John (or indeed anytime between 1180 and 1247) and was clipped to remove a significant amount of silver, then released back into circulation as one penny, thereby contributing an illegal profit to the clipper. As this activity takes away the outer edge of the coin, geometry informs that a large proportion can be removed – in this example half the weight of the original. Clipping of hammered coins was widespread in Britain and Europe for many centuries. The French billon (silver/copper alloy) dizain was struck in 1488 at Rouen under Charles VIII (1483–1498) and originally weighed around 2.4 g. This example has lost nearly all of the encircling legend and is a paltry 1.36 g. Even coins not made of good silver were clipped. (18 mm, 19 mm and 1.40 g, 11 mm and 0.69 g, 19 mm.)

the consequence of someone with access to punches battering one or two out for fun – further complicate the matter. Most unofficial (and many official) countermarks will have had a limited local circulation for which all records are now lost (if they ever existed). Some of these unknown countermarks can be quite intriguing, though we can but speculate where and how they might have been employed. Some are perhaps more deliberately obscure as they were issued in contexts which may have been less than socially acceptable. However, all of them meant something to someone.

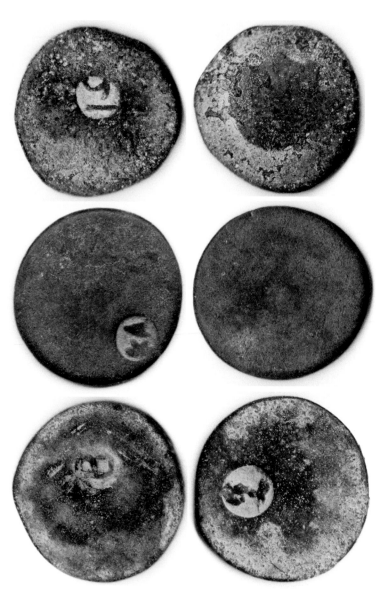

A currency in crisis, Petra – 'The Rose-Red City in the Desert', in Jordan – in the late third century. Until the currency reforms devised by Emperor Diocletian had percolated through the system after 294 a desperate shortage of coinage befell this region. Petra resorted to countermarking extremely worn coins. The 'B' countermark on the first appears to be denomination mark. The figure on the reverse cannot be the number 2 as Hindu-Arabic numerals had not reached the Middle East at this time and its orientation as shown here may be inaccurate. The second with 'KA' may inform that it was produced by the town's administrative body. The third, from the same source as the previous two, is unknown – its orientation may also be incorrect. All three demonstrate the dismal state of small change at the glorious rock-cut metropolis in this period. (c. 24 mm.)

Advertising countermarks by two prolific self-publicists in the late nineteenth century. Allan Dahl of Denmark advertised his firm as the 'Bureau for Permanent Advertising'. Taking his own advice he countermarked many Norwegian and, as here, Swedish five öre coins, these being the same dimensions as a Danish five öre. Presumably they entered the Danish marketplace as 'unofficial' currency but avoided any laws relating to defacement of coinage. John Burton's Old Curiosity Shop, Falmouth, was a famed Aladdin's cave of treasures and curios from around the world. He relied on sailors for his stock and a mariner must have brought back a large job lot of Japanese four mon coins for him which he then countermarked. These he subsequently handed out to seamen as a reminder that he was always in the market for any unusual and beautiful treasures they could bring back from their voyages to distant lands. (27 mm.)

Unidentified issuers. At the top left is a lead blank countermarked with a standing figure of Helios, most likely in Sicily, probably fourth century BC, presumably to produce a lead token. Beneath this is a worn George II farthing from 1754, on which a sun countermark has been punched over the head of Britannia. The British 'cartwheel' penny of 1797 was countermarked twice by 'I·P', then subsequently by 'M·P 1804'. Is this a trader's token, passed down from father to a son who took over the business that year? The 1862 penny was countermarked by the obverse sustaining a heavy blow, producing the high-relief design on the reverse. A horse and rider along with three hounds implies a fox-hunting theme. The final mystery piece shows two marks on either a copper blank or a totally worn coin. Its provenance is utterly unknown, both as regards country of issue and date of production, though nineteenth to early twentieth century is the most probable range. Imagination can take over when no information survives: is this a moon next to an apple containing a cider barrel, with a stem and single leaf of this fruit within the inwardly curved top of the oval shape? One suggestion is that it could be an apple-picker's token from 'Moon Farm'. (22 mm–36 mm.)

Commerce in less than socially acceptable establishments? Bringing to mind the 'luncheon voucher scandal' of the late 1970s, when gentlemen paid for certain 'services' using luncheon vouchers in lieu of actual money, here we have two unknown countermarks: the first on an 1806 halfpenny of George III, the second on a German pfennig of 1900. The British example may indicate some local disdain for regal authority, though the position of the initial countermark, applied so securely over the king's head, might suggest it was impressed in France during or soon after the Napoleonic Wars. (18 mm–28 mm.)

Jettons

The term jetton (or jeton) derives from the French verb *jeter*, in the sense of 'to push' or 'to cast', and was a reckoning or casting-counter allowing for quicker calculations by royal administrators, bankers and merchants in the mediaeval period than could be achieved with the cumbersome Roman numerals then in use. The earliest recorded examples are considered to date from the reign of French king Louis IX (1226–1270). They soon became popular across most of Europe. In the fifteenth and sixteenth centuries their manufacture centred on France, especially Tournai (now in Belgium). The earliest French types followed regal and church symbolism and commonly carried the Latin inscription *Ave Maria Gratia Plena* – 'Hail Mary, Full of Grace'. These were followed by increasingly varied types. By the late sixteenth century jettons were also produced in great numbers in Nuremberg, Germany.

With the rise in dominance of the easier-to-use Hindu-Arabic numbering system jettons became less an instrument of calculation. In France they transformed into an exhibition of the medallist's art, while German manufacturers tended to transfer their interest towards making counters for games – their descendants can be found in 'amusement arcades' across the world today. In England, jettons-as-cash has a history stretching back to Plantagenet times.

Jettons commonly found in England. Three early French examples showing the enthroned French king (*c.* 1270), the Châtel-Tournois (*c.* 1300) and the shield of France (*c.* 1400). In the early 1960s the second jetton was spotted in a recently ploughed field in north-east Derbyshire. Presumably it had been used as small change in the area prior to its loss, probably in the late 1300s. After being rediscovered its life as currency briefly began anew when it was given by the finder to local numismatist Bunty the Barber as payment for a haircut. It subsequently passed into the hands of the author when Bunty encouraged this young lad's interest in all matters numismatic. Here we also have two stock German jettons from the sixteenth century or early seventeenth, both with reverses showing the *reichsapfel* (imperial orb). The first obverse has three open crowns and three lys arranged alternately. The latter is the lion of St Mark. (24 mm–27 mm.)

Tokens

The range of types and variation in use of metal discs (sometimes paper or other materials) described as tokens (occasionally, checks) is enormous. Often they are a form of guarantee as their intrinsic value is far lower than their stated value. All modern currencies and small denomination copper, bronze, lead or pewter coins since ancient times are token money.

Mainstream tokens may be considered to be those issued privately by such as towns and traders in periods when the central authority failed to deliver an adequate supply of small change. They were issued on the promise that they would be redeemed for normal currency at a later time. In the absence of these tokens, local commerce could have been almost impossible in societies that customarily based both large and small transactions on coins.

More generally a token is often taken to include any coin-like piece which has a particular function. Although they are known from Greek and Roman times and into the Middle Ages, the rise of the Industrial Age witnessed a bewildering eruption of these issues with applications in quite varied circumstances. While some were issued by governments, most were constrained within specific local environments, having no value outside of this. As with many countermarks, these tokens operated on a need-to-know basis. This implies in-group acceptance, though it could become a form of control, limiting the ability of individuals to stray outside of demarcated boundaries, be that a factory, a shop or a pub. Again, in a similar manner to countermarks, little documentary or oral evidence survives clarifying in what ways these tokens had value and it is likely that the rules of how individuals interacted with them varied from establishment to establishment. In small-scale enterprises, such as a beer outlet in an out-of-the-way village, some quite idiosyncratic systems were likely to have been devised and practiced. Unlike countermarks these are complete coin-like entities and their manufacture would tend to be more expensive, suggesting that their role was of a higher sort. However, countermarks and other adaptations are frequently found on tokens, somewhat blurring the distinction between them.

Church tokens have a history stretching back to the early Middle Ages, from whence they functioned in diverse roles and comprised many different types. In France – where they were known as *méreaux* – one variety entitled clergy to receive an amount of bread or other food, part of which was later distributed among the poor. Another type was given as a reward to clergy who attended particular services. Was this for ritualistic purposes, or does it imply that certain members of the ministry would not have shown up for these religious observances? The *Catholic Encyclopaedia* suggests the latter when it states that these tokens were also known as '*jetons de présence*' with a primary purpose 'to secure the due attendance of the canons at the cathedral offices'. The token of 1526 from St Omer Church is of this type. The reverse legend 'PRESENTIBUS DABITUR' – 'Will be present' – tends to support the encyclopaedia's contention.

A further variety of church token used within the Catholic tradition is represented by this example from St Lambert's Cathedral, Liège, of 1686. It was handed out during Mass not to clergy, but directly to the poor – those who sat on the benches furthest from the pulpit. When the church bells sounded the recipients would redeem the tokens – proof that they had been present for the service – to collect bread, passed out through one of the church windows. These pieces might also be regarded as inducement, though a gentler inference is that they played a part within a ritual of church-giving. The legend 'ANNIVERSARIUM' (anniversary) indicates that they were allotted during services dedicated to St Lambert (*c.* 640–705).

Bread and the grain used in its making enjoy a special place in many cultures, both as a staple foodstuff and as an embodiment of religious belief. Over the centuries situations have arisen for which tokens have been preferred to standard currency for certain dealings regarding these fundamental resources. Almsgiving at the cathedral of Liège is one such example. The two tokens here from Germany tell of mills and grain and times of desperate need.

Local mills were central to village life and to farms scattered in open country. In pastoral regions grain for cattle feed might also be supplied through the agency of the mill, as here from 1658, issued at Hildesheim, a town in Lower Saxony. They were produced to enable its citizens to purchase cattle grain (wheat in this case) in a standardised manner. Higher value pieces were made in bronze, while the lower value ones were formed in a baser metal such as lead. Above the date on the reverse were representations of grains of wheat indicating for how much the token could be redeemed – the example illustrated with its two grains was worth the equivalent of around eight gallons (36 litres) of wheat.

Some 290 km south-west of Hildesheim lies the town of Elberfeld. In the 1700s it was a centre of textile manufacturing, with most of the finished products being sold to France. With the onset of the French Revolution this market fell away and unemployment and poverty began to increase. On the other side of the planet in 1815 a geological phenomenon would considerably amplify these difficulties. Mount Tambora lies on the small Indonesian island of Sumbawa. Its eruption that year was one of the most powerful in recorded history and it changed climatic conditions to such an extent that 1816 became known as the 'year without a summer'. Harvests failed in many areas around the world, including Elberfeld, which then had to import grain. Unhappily for those people already under pressure the consequent inflation left many without their daily bread. Rather than leave the inhabitants to deal with this as best as they might the Elberfelder Kornverein (Elberfeld Grain Association) was formed and fifty-six of the more wealthy citizens drew shares amounting to around 74,000 thalers. A hundred other citizens raised another 50,000 thalers and the project was guaranteed. This money was used to

Copper church tokens. *Méreau* of XII (12) deniers from 1526. The obverse legend reads: 'MO ECC SANTI AUDOMARI' (Church money of Saint Omer Church). A well-used token from St Lambert's Cathedral, Liège, 1686, showing his holy relics which were housed in the early eighth-century shrine dedicated to him, around which the cathedral was built. The indistinct reverse legend reads 'ECCLESI LEODI' (Church of Liège). (18 mm–23 mm.)

buy cheaper grain and flour from less effected regions, with the price difference being passed on to the more destitute in the population. Regrettably some bakers attempted to take advantage of this situation and sold underweight loaves or added foreign matter to the mix. In order to stop this fraud tokens were issued which set the balance for an equivalent amount of flour for each loaf. The sunshine returned during 1817, the situation improved and the work of the association was no longer necessary. The story did not end there, however, for it had made a profit of 13,000 thalers, with which the town's first hospital was built.

Tokens of one type or another have been part of the German beer-drinking landscape for centuries, though it was from around 1860 that they became commonly part of daily business, used in large quantities in bars – many of which were also small breweries. A number of explanations have been presented for how they were employed. Probably the primary one was for pre-payment of beer – either through the waiting staff or at the counter – which were then presented when beer was ordered. A secondary function describes them as 'coupons' from competitions or promotions when a certain quantity of beer crates or bottles were bought – buy a crate of beer, get a token for a free bottle. After the First World War, when the German economy was in chaos and inflation rife, beer could bought in advance through purchasing tokens which would be redeemed later for a glass of the stuff, even when prices had increased dramatically. Similar strategies were also devised for bread and other commodities.

Before the Second World War Canada imported many items of food, but factors such as military action on the high seas meant certain countries no longer being able to export food, and supplies being needed for Canadian troops forced rationing on the nation. When it was first introduced in 1942, families were given a book of coupons which could be exchanged for meat and other essentials. However, not everyone was part of a family and those who lived alone or as a couple had to forfeit a whole coupon for a lesser ration, or take home more than they could use. To resolve this difficulty meat tokens were issued from September 1945 to March 1947, where eight were worth one coupon. If only half a meat ration, for example, was wanted or allowed, then for every coupon four of these tokens were handed out as change.

Square lead token from Hildesheim, 1658, for purchasing cattle grain, showing the town's arms and two grains of wheat. Elberfeld Grain Association bread token, 1817. For those interested in linguistic variations, bread here is given as *brod*; the current German term is *brot*. (24 mm–25 mm.)

Good for a glass (or a half) of beer. Carl Jamin, before 1900, 'To the German Kaiser', from Oberursel, Frankfurt am Main. Heinrich Theiss, around 1920, brewery beer deposit from Herborn, a village in Rhineland-Palatinate. The brewery-guesthouse Herold, unknown date, though probably nineteenth century, from Büchenbach, a village in Upper Franconia, Bavaria. This concern today advertises that 'brewing, bar and baking rights have existed since 1568'. With a medieval king raising a glass, a later brewery bar token from Frankfurt. (21 mm–23 mm.)

Canadian ration book from the 1940s and a page of unused coupons. Meat ration token made of wood. (13.5 mm by 8.5 mm, 22 mm.)

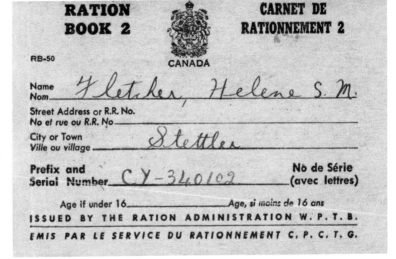

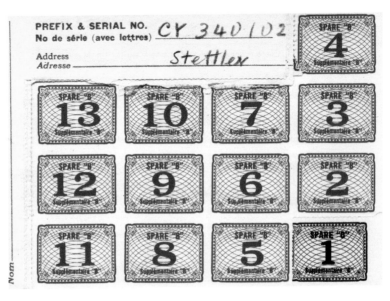

Part Two

Britain 150 BC to AD 2019

Celt and Roman

Coinage arrived late in Britain, as it did in other European regions remote from the Mediterranean sphere of influence. In the early part of the second century BC a new empire was rising in the far south, pushing its borders and its use of currency northwards: Rome. Gold coins from northern Gaul first landed on our south-eastern shores around 150 BC, though exactly why they did so is unknown. What is acknowledged is that cross-Channel contacts, exchanges and movements of peoples had been actively pursued since at least the Bronze Age – Llandudno's axes being one example of this. In a number of respects these coins may have functioned in a manner similar to precious metals and objects of value in other pre-coin societies, such as reciprocal gift exchanges between elites, for reinforcing alliances or for paying mercenaries. Whatever their function, these and subsequent gold coins minted in Britain were decidedly not small change, though they do demonstrate the vibrant craftsmanship of Celtic art forms and introduced the concept of currency to the country. Although the tribes of Britain were unsuspecting of where this might lead, they were being drawn closer to the world of Rome.

The first Celtic coins produced in Britain were cast potin (copper/tin) issues from Kent, *c.* 120 BC, though, again, why this occurred is not clear. These imitated Gaulish coins, which were based on prototypes from Massilia (Marseille), originally a Greek colony on the Mediterranean coast. The first British locally made gold coins also appeared in Kent *c.* 70 BC. A nascent market economy was developing which required the production of smaller change and a range of denominations, including middling value silver coins, began to be issued. Coinage gradually extended to neighbouring tribes, along the south coast to Dorset, north to the Midlands and into East Anglia and to the Humber. The rest of Britain remained outside of this currency-using zone.

In the early years of the first century AD, Cunobeline (Shakespeare's Cymbeline) unified the tribes of the Trinovantes and Catuvellauni north of the Thames and held territories in Kent. His expansion of power was to be a concern to the powers that be in Rome, who, of course, were aware of Britain following the excursions of Julius Caesar in 55 and 54 BC. The Celts, having no written language of their own, adopted the Latin alphabet for their coins. British independence began to unravel further when Verica, ruler of the Atrebates and Regni (Berkshire and Hampshire), fled to Rome in AD 42/3 seeking aid from Emperor Claudius (AD 41–54) against the expansionist policies of Cunobeline.

Golden Celts and horses. Top left: Gallic-Belgic quarter stater, imported into Britain *c.* 150–50 BC. The gold stater, top right, was issued in Kent around 65 BC and has the same underlying design as the Gallo-Belgic issue, though its component elements have become increasingly disjointed. Cunobeline's stater here, with an ear of corn and a frisky horse, has the mint named on the obverse, 'CAMVL' for Camulodunum (Colchester), and his name, 'CVN' (Cunobeline), on the reverse. A vine leaf divides the first four letters on the stater of Verica, *c.* AD 10–40, probably struck at Calleva (Silchester). The reverse shows a Celtic horseman. (*c.* 14 mm–17 mm.) (Courtesy Museums Victoria)

The cast potin issue from Kent, *c.* 120 BC, presents a bust and a bull butting left. From this original prototype the series quickly degraded – or was adapted for ease of mass-production – to a far simpler type, as shown by the second cast coin issued around 100 BC. In the far west of the currency-issuing zone the Durotriges, centred on Dorset, traded directly south across the wider stretch of channel to Armorica – western Gaul and the Channel Islands. Between *c.* 75 and 50 BC Armorican coinage comprised billon staters with head and stylised horse. Coinage of the Durotriges initially followed the trends in the rest of southern Britain, but soon developed their own distinctive style. Their white gold staters issued by 58 BC with the abstract head of Apollo and disjointed horse rapidly deteriorated to billon issues (which may have been silver plated), probably due to the loss of trade across the channel, where Julius Caesar was at large. He is depicted on this bronze sestertius from Italy, struck after his death by nephew Octavian in 38 BC. (14 mm–30 mm). (The first image courtesy Chris Rudd Ltd, the second courtesy Museums Victoria.)

The first silver coin here, undeniably Celtic in form, has been attributed (uncertainly) to Queen Boudicca (Boadicea) of the Norfolk-based Iceni tribe, who led an ultimately doomed revolt against Roman intervention in British affairs. The silver unit with the Celtic boar on the reverse dates from around AD 15, an issue of Verica. The last, a highly Romanised silver unit with the head of Hercules and an eagle standing on a snake, was struck *c.* AD 35 for Epaticcus, probably a brother of Cunobeline. (11 mm–13 mm.) (First image courtesy Museums Victoria)

Claudius and his army landed in Britain in AD 43, though the emperor stayed in this barbarian northern land for only sixteen days. At first rebellions and a certain anguish greeted their presence. However, the southern province, comprising much of what is now England and Wales, would become a relatively peaceful land of towns, villas and commerce with a uniform, empire-wide currency. In the troublesome outer regions a strong military presence of forts and garrisons was to develop. Scotland was never conquered by the Romans and remained quite separate, if frequent Scottish and Pictish raids across the border for plunder are overlooked.

As the Roman influence spread across the land a state of affairs began to arise which would prevail repeatedly up to the nineteenth century: namely, a shortage of small change. Probably fuelled by the economic prospects of dealing with military garrisons, a full monetary economy became a necessity. This resulted in a dearth of coins in many areas, with the consequence that forgeries began to appear. The earliest are reasonable copies of the originals and may have enjoyed official sanction, though these soon degenerated into smaller and cruder copies.

As the southern regions developed a fully Romanised way of life, with commerce now across the Channel and into the vast empire, the northern areas remained a vexing problem. One solution to this was begun in AD 122 during the emperor's visit to this region: Hadrian's Wall. This stretched from the Tyne to Solway Firth. With trouble persisting, a new wall, begun in 142, was built from the Forth to the Clyde on the orders of Antoninus Pius (AD 138–192). This was abandoned in the mid-160s and the edge of empire returned to Hadrian's construction, where it remained, notwithstanding repeated attacks and breaches, until the early fifth century. Coins celebrating victories in Britain had been minted in Rome since the days of Claudius. One, however, is likely to have been produced by a temporary or travelling mint near the northern border for Antoninus Pius.

The period of the *Pax Romana* (Roman Peace) from AD 68 to 180 was to be the highpoint of the empire. From this period onwards attacks on the northern borders by barbarian tribes and the seemingly never-ending conflict with Persian rulers escalated. At the centre insurgents seized imperial power; they themselves were usually soon deposed or assassinated. Against this background Postumus, governor of Upper and Lower Germany, was proclaimed emperor by his troops in AD 260. So began fourteen years of the 'Gallic Empire', a territory which included Britain and Spain. In this chaos

Above: With a provenance of Brittany, the first forgery of a coin of Augustus (27 BC–AD 14) tells that this problem was not confined to Britain. The second is an official Rome issue of Claudius with the reverse showing Minerva. The third, from Britain, is a reasonable copy of this, though the fourth, with its retrograde letters and crude workmanship, is anything but a good copy. (20 mm–27 mm.) (Claudius with permission of wildwinds.com)

Below: Denarius of Claudius celebrating his British victory, with triumphal arch inscribed 'DE BRITANN' surmounted by an equestrian statue between two trophies. The denarius of Hadrian (AD 117–138), with Oceanus holding an anchor, was issued in Rome in 122. The coin of Antoninus Pius displaying a dejected Britannia seated on a pile of rocks was minted near to his wall, though was somewhat crudely made. (17 mm–25 mm.) (Claudius with permission of wildwinds.com)

the economy collapsed and by the early 270s forgeries (or imitations struck under desperate conditions?) became rife. The quality of these 'barbarous radiates' was often staggeringly crude.

The disintegrating empire was brought under control and stabilised by Diocletian (AD 284–305). In AD 294 he reformed the coinage and began the first steps to dividing the empire into two halves: one based on Byzantium, the second on Rome. The focus of the Roman Empire was shifting east. In Britain at this time rebellion was once again afoot. Emperor Maximianus (AD 286–305) appointed Carausius to clear the waterway between Gaul and Britain of Saxon and Frankish pirates, using Boulogne as his base. Unfortunately Carausius turned native and became a pirate himself. Rather than face the wrath of the emperor he sailed to Britain, defeated the governor, and assumed control of the island (AD 287–293). He lost Boulogne in AD 293 and soon after was murdered by his chief minister, Allectus (AD 293–296). Having taken over the task of recovering the province, future emperor Constantius I (AD 305–306) invaded Britain and the rebellion was quelled when Allectus was killed on the battlefield. Two mints operated during this period: London and another designated with the mintmark 'C', probably Camulodunum (Colchester). These were the first official mints to operate in Roman Britain and were maintained by subsequent emperors to AD 325.

Constantius died at York in AD 306 while repelling an invasion by the Picts. His troops immediately proclaimed his son Constantine as emperor, though over the ensuing years many counter-claims to his power had to be confronted. In one of these Constantine was threatened by a revolt led by Maxentius. The two forces came together at Milvian Bridge outside Rome in AD 312. Though heavily outnumbered, Constantine prevailed. It is claimed that on the day of the battle he had been aided by divine intervention as

Official issues (originals for most 'barbarous radiates') of Gallic Empire emperors: Claudius II, Gothicus (AD 268–270), the first issued during his reign, the second after his death; Tetricus I (AD 270–273); and his son, Tetricus II (AD 270–273). (*c.* 18 mm.) (Tetricus I with permission of wildwinds.com)

Above: 'Barbarous radiates'. (6 mm–21 mm.)

Below: The first is an antoninianus of Carausius, the last is the same denomination for Allectus, both from London. The forgeries between them suggest that their inspiration came from coins of Carausius. (17 mm–22 mm.) (The two official issues with permission of wildwinds.com)

he had ordered his troops to adorn their shields with the chi-rho symbol, the first two letters of Christ's name written in the Greek alphabet (XP). In AD 313 Constantine and co-emperor Licinius issued the Edict of Milan, granting tolerance to all religions, including Christianity.

With the closure of the London mint small change was once more dependent on transfers across the Channel. After the death of Constantine in AD 337, the empire was again in chaos and forgeries filled the resulting shortage of everyday coinage. For a brief period the London mint operated under the rebel Magnus Maximus (AD 383–388) – celebrated in Wales as Macsen Wledig – who became emperor of the western provinces. Germanic inroads and conquests in the Western Empire had escalated during the fourth century. When asked for assistance by Britain in AD 410 Emperor Honorius replied that the islanders should arrange for their own defence. Britain ceased to be a Roman province and coinage disappeared as Roman ways of working quickly faded away.

Above: Mint of London – the first three of Constantine, the fourth for his son and junior co-emperor Crispus (AD 317–326). The altars are inscribed 'votis', which relates to vows made by the emperor. The building on the third represents a camp gate. (18 mm–20 mm.)

Below: In 330 Constantine dedicated Byzantium as the new Christian capital of the empire, changing its name to Constantinopolis. A commemorative coinage was issued over the next few years depicting a personification of the city. A comparative issue in the west represented Roma with the reverse showing the foundation myth of Romulus and Remus. The first two coins are official issues. The two British-found forgeries are hybrids, copied from the obverse of the Constantinopolis emission with an Urbs Roma reverse. Although official mints throughout time have often employed different die cutters for obverse and reverse types, forgeries tend to be the work of a single person; however, the last example intriguingly seems to have been produced by two individuals as the cutting of the obverse and reverse dies are quite different. (11 mm–19 mm.)

Above: Early Christian iconography. After the death of Constantine I his sons Constantine II and Constantius II issued an extensive series of coins for the deified emperor. This example from Alexandria (AD 337–340) shows a veiled Constantine; on the reverse he drives a quadriga and his right hand reaches up towards the hand of God. The following two forgeries bear the chi-rho device, making them very early references to Christianity. (12 mm–15 mm.)

Below: Unsophisticated British forgeries *c.* AD 350 or later. (8 mm–11 mm.)

The first coin here of Magnus Maximus is from an unknown mint, the second from Constantia (Arles), AD 383–386. The rather charming reverse of the first shows a kneeling figure which at first sight appears to be a young prince, though is in fact a female. The figure on the right (holding a globe on which stands Victory with wreath) is the emperor dressed in military attire – but presented with a decidedly feminine deportment. In terms of style, this image might not look out of place in late medieval or Renaissance artwork. Notwithstanding its worn condition, the other coin displays a more masculine portrayal of the emperor. (*c.* 23 mm.)

Anglo-Saxons and Normans

With the demise of the Roman Empire, western Europe was embroiled in unrestrained mass migration, wars and the comprehensive subjugation and displacement of indigenous populations. Petty kingdoms rose and fell and a couple of centuries or more passed before a tentative stability returned to the region. In Britain Teutonic peoples, loosely defined as 'Anglo-Saxon', had settled from the third century, as members of the Roman army and as mercenaries invited to intervene in local wars. With the leaving of Rome a trickle became a flood. The seaborne invaders advanced over the southern parts of the island and in these areas an 'English' language and culture came to dominate. Cities were forsaken and literacy for the population at large became a thing of the past. Coins also disappeared and a local barter and credit economy once again prevailed.

The first coins to reappear in what was now Anglo-Saxon southern England were of gold, imported in the late sixth century from the Merovingian kingdom in France. Native coin production began around AD 630, small gold coins initially imitating Continental emissions so as to further trade with what are now the Low Countries. Silver coins emerged by about AD 675 and came to predominate in British currencies. With rare exceptions gold coins were not issued again until the fourteenth century and – with the exception of Northumberland – it took until the seventeenth century for copper coins to reappear. Clearly, the social and economic landscape had changed in Anglo-Saxon times, one which (put in probably simplistic terms) involved alterations in forms of tenancy and credit systems, and in relationships with ones 'betters'. The story of small change largely disappears from the narrative for a further 400 years.

The coinage of Britain was influenced again by mainland Europe when silver pennies began to be issued. These imitated deniers were minted initially in AD 755 for Pepin, king of the Franks. In AD 930 a sheep would cost in the order of one shilling (twelve pennies); by 1300 the same amount would purchase a pair of shoes. With no small change being issued, the dearth was partly resolved by the application of shears and cut halves and quarters appeared by the tenth century. The penny tradition continued beyond 1066 when the last English king, Harold II, and England itself fell to the Normans, as soon-to-be King William I was quite familiar with currency of this type.

Above: Early Anglo-Saxon silver coins. The first from *c*. AD 680–710 was struck in various regions of south-eastern and eastern England with radiate bust, reverse TOTII on a standard. This type resembles Roman coinages of the third and fourth centuries. The once-plated copper core is a forgery of a type issued *c*. AD 710–760 with two diademed heads face-to-face (or perhaps more accurately, nose-to-nose) and four birds around a cross. It was found in Wiltshire. Criminal activities were thus soon to take advantage of the possibilities offered by the re-emergence of coins. (*c*. 10 mm.)

Below: The penny would be virtually the only denomination produced in England for almost five centuries. Cuthred (AD 798–807), king of Kent; Alfred the Great (AD 871–899), London; Harold II (1066), London, within the rectangle, 'PAX' (PEACE) – the same propaganda (or optimism) as presented in the circles around the cross on the penny of William the Conqueror (1066–1087). (*c*. 19 mm.) (Courtesy Museums Victoria)

Above: In the days before the Vikings took troublesome interest in the area (the 870s), a silver sceatta coinage was issued by the kings of Northumbria in the eighth century. By *c.* 810 these had transformed into base silver and copper-alloy stycas: small-denomination coins of practical benefit. The styca on the left an issue of Æthelred II (AD 841–843/4), followed by one of Redwulf (AD 843/4). Eanbald II was Archbishop of York, AD 796–835. The final two are irregular issues with blundered legends from *c.* AD 843–855. (*c.* 11 mm.) (The first three courtesy Museums Victoria)

Below: Two halfpennies (obverse, then reverse) carefully halved along the axis of the cross: English king Æthelred II 'the Unready' (AD 978–1016), Exeter, and Cnut (1016–1035), Lincoln. The complete York penny of Edward the Confessor (1042–1066) might raise suspicions that skulduggery was wrought in the production of the cut farthing. At first sight (and probably in practice in the eleventh century) it appears acceptable. However, on the right the quarter has been repeated four times so that the outer diameter matches with Edward's penny. If all four 'quarters' of the original had been fashioned in a similar manner then someone made a nice profit with the silver left over. (Full coins *c.* 19 mm.) (Cnut half and Edward penny courtesy Museums Victoria)

From Henry II to Richard III

The medieval period was not one of stagnation but of progression, with developments in agriculture, the founding of small towns serving their surrounding agrarian landscapes, rising populations and the fostering of a more moneyed economy. London became the capital for the royal court and for merchants: it handled a least a third of all overseas British trade by 1300 as links with mainland Europe were strengthened. By the late thirteenth century English domination of Wales and Scotland was gathering pace. The Crusades became an additional foreign venture, bringing novel alliances, unfamiliar conflict and fresh ideas. England had entered a new phase. However, ancient methods remained important for the lower levels of society, which comprised the majority of the population. The marketplace remained firmly based in traditional practices of barter and credit, with any coinage available being used to periodically pay off accrued debts.

England's money did not remain static during these times. Henry II (1154–1189) introduced new types of penny, first in 1154 ('cross-and crosslets') and in 1180 the 'short cross' type. The latter variety remained virtually unchanged up to 1247, during the reigns of Richard I, John, and Henry III, all with Henricus as the king's name. Henry III (1216–1272) produced the 'long cross' penny in 1247, a design which it was hoped would thwart clippers. Edward I (1272–1307) continued these types until 1279, when a major recoinage was embarked upon, minting coins in his own name and introducing a novel four-pence coin, the groat (from the French, *gros*), though it was not a success and was not minted again until 1351 for Edward III (1327–1377).

In all this there is little mention of small change. Some round halfpennies had been produced under Henry I (1100–1135) but these and round farthings were not issued further until the time of King John (1199–1216). Into this vacuum appeared tokens of lead, pewter and other materials, supplied by individuals, merchants, farmers, and by institutions such as the Church. These remained part of the darker economy until the nineteenth century. Imported jettons, especially those mass-produced in France and Germany, also took on a role ensuring that the little things in life could be purchased. How else could a simple flagon of cider be enjoyed in a thirteenth-century tavern when a gallon cost a halfpenny?

Short-cross pennies in the name of Henry II, the second minted by moneyer Ilger in London. (*c*.18 mm.)

Long cross pennies, the first two for Edward I, from London and Bristol. The penny of Edward III has been clipped slightly, the following two for Edward IV more so. The last is no larger than a halfpenny of Edward I. (20 mm–14 mm.) (Apart from Edward I, London mint, courtesy Museums Victoria)

Two round halfpennies and two farthings. The second is an issue for Edward IV, the other three for Edward I. (14 mm–10 mm.)

Four cut halfpennies from the reign of Henry III. (*c.* 17 mm.)

Four cut farthings, the first of a cross-and-crosslet penny of Henry II, the next two (both suspiciously small) of pennies of Henry III – the fourth can only be described as a fragment masquerading as a farthing. The clipped and cut three-quarters of a penny from later in the period could have been deliberately formed to produce a three-farthing coin, or is what remained after a farthing had been removed, prior to its loss. (Three-farthing, 16 mm.)

English jettons, the first with a facing head mimicking the standard design on pennies, probably issued under Edward I, the second with two lions passant for Edward II. Although produced for use with counting boards, such pieces were readily pressed into service as small change. (19 mm.)

The only 'small change' available in local communities? Lead/pewter tokens with crosses and geometric designs, dating from the medieval period to the sixteenth century. (9 mm–21 mm.)

The first lead/pewter token shows a stylised water bird with a peck-marked reverse. The following appears to show a terrestrial bird. These may be early in the series. The last two with initials are later and are probably farm tokens. (13 mm–28 mm.)

The two lead/pewter ecclesiastical tokens on the left were likely issued by monasteries to pay artisans and probably date to the later medieval period. They were nicknamed 'abbot's money' and had small, local circulations. The first was retrieved from the Thames. The paschal lamb on the second is somewhat crudely produced. The two cast lead-alloy 'Boy Bishop' tokens are ecclesiastical issues from the Suffolk area – particularly Bury St Edmunds – in the late fifteenth century up to around 1535. They resemble contemporary denominations, pennies and groats. It was customary for churches and abbeys to elect a choirboy as Boy Bishop from St Nicholas' Day (6 December) to Holy Innocents' Day (28 December). The Boy Bishop distributed the tokens to the congregation and they were probably exchanged for alms or sweetmeats. The wide area of East Anglia and into eastern England where they are found suggests they also saw service as small change. (12 mm–28 mm.)

Coiners, Clippers and Castration in the Middle Ages

Coining crimes throughout history have attracted individuals from across the social spectrum. Moneyers were high-ranking officials, sometimes ecclesiastical, licensed by the monarch to strike coin. They could abuse this positon by issuing lightweight or debased specimens, and from Norman times onwards many sought to defraud the royal personage. A mass conviction of moneyers ensued in 1125, where the penalty included having their right hands cut off and castration. Notwithstanding these punishments, still these crimes persisted. The next major coining crisis occurred in 1279, which led to the execution of some 269 Jews and twenty-nine Christians in London for clipping, though it may be questioned whether this was solely the cause of Edward I's assault.

Those accused were mainly involved in moneylending, or were goldsmiths and similar, so possessed wealth which was naturally acquired by the Crown. It was also in 1279 that he taxed the clergy at a higher rate than normal to help pay for his campaign against the Welsh. Clipping was acknowledged to be widespread among all classes, or at least those individuals who had ready access to coins and the wherewithal to disperse the outcomes of their activity.

The Tudors

Towards the end of the fifteenth century the world was becoming quite different to anything that had gone before. Voyages of exploration by Spanish and Portuguese navigators were discovering sea passages to distant continents; colonisation, religious conversion, exploitation and worldwide trading networks followed swiftly, including the beginning of the intercontinental slave trade and increased piracy. In northern Europe Christianity was soon to be transformed with the rise of divergent ideologies and churches.

Henry VII (1485–1509), the victor of the Wars of the Roses, largely kept aloof from foreign campaigns. His main concerns were to bring stability to the land, found a dynasty, and amass money rather than recklessly spend it. On his groat, which had survived virtually unchanged since the days of Edward I, the traditional crown was replaced with an arched imperial crown. In 1504 the design was radically changed; the king was shown in profile and the reverse now had an armorial design superimposed on the long cross. The smallest change, halfpennies and farthings, continued the medieval tradition; the new 'sovereign' penny now presented the king enthroned.

Henry's first son, Arthur, predeceased him and it fell to the next to continue the dynasty. Henry VIII (1509–1547) was far more cavalier than his father and embroiled himself in foreign adventures. Henry married his elder brother's widow, Katherine of Aragon, shortly after his accession. The story is well known of Katherine's inability to bear him a son and heir and the ensuing divorce, followed by five further wives. Henry had been raised a Catholic and the circumstances surrounding his attempts to gain a divorce led ultimately to a split with the Church in Rome. The resultant Dissolution of the Monasteries (1536–40) raised substantial financial gains for the king and his associates. Nevertheless, towards the end of his reign, with his father's money spent, his personal extravagance, and with rising inflation, he remained in serious financial difficulties: in 1544 coinage was debased and individual denominations grew smaller. Farthings were effectively abandoned.

The young Edward VI (1547–1553), a zealous Protestant, tried to ensure that Lady Jane Grey succeeded him, but in this he was unsuccessful and the throne passed to his half-sister Mary (1553–1558), daughter of Katherine of Aragon. She is probably best known for her aggressive attempt to reverse the English Reformation. Her marriage to Philip of Spain, a Catholic, in 1554 was unpopular among her subjects and her religious policies resulted in deep-seated resentment. Spanish attention to England, threatened invasions and armadas came to naught during the reign of Elizabeth I (1558–1603). At the end of her reign England entered the seventeenth century with a new self-confidence and its overseas status raised. At home the population had risen to over 4 million by 1601, a greater than 30 per cent increase since 1541, and this brought with it rising poverty. Economic stagnation was apparent and inflation was a perennial problem. The 'lower orders' saw their standard of living decline.

The first two groats look almost identical, yet they are separated in time by almost seventy years. The first was struck in Calais (then an English possession) in 1427–1430 for Henry VI, the second in London, 1499–1502, for Henry VII. The third, a London issue of 1505–1509 for Henry VII, is quite novel with its profile bust and armorial shield. His smallest change, farthings and halfpence, continued the old tradition, as here with his London halfpenny. A large gold pound piece was first issued in Henry's reign; this presented the sovereign sat on a backless throne – henceforth the name of gold pound coins: sovereigns. The penny's obverse was a derivative of this design. (*c.* 12 mm–25 mm.)

The farthing of Henry VIII is a miserable 7 mm in diameter, and users found them most inconvenient. The second is a debased groat issued towards the end of Henry's life. Although the following halfgroat has Henry's name and image, it was struck posthumously during the early part of the reign of Edward VI. Edward's threepence has the figures 'III' to the right of his bust; to the left a rose further aided the public to differentiate this denomination from groats. (7 mm–24 mm.) (Halfpenny, groat and threepence courtesy of Museums Victoria)

Small change throughout the Tudor period was never plentiful. With a debasement of the coinage under Henry VIII and a subsequent reduction in size of the increasingly impractical smallest denominations, a chronic shortage ensued. Moneyers were reluctant to strike tedious little silver coins as the work involved was proportionally greater than for larger denominations, so they used up their quotas of silver to the detriment of everyday coins. Base metal coins, which would have alleviated the difficulty, were considered beneath the dignity of the Crown. Inevitably, shopkeepers and others resorted to issuing – or issued in greater quantities than previously – unofficial tokens. The small change of Merrie England was in a dire state.

The first groat was issued before Mary's marriage to Philip. The shilling, struck after her marriage, has the somewhat tactless inscription: 'Philip and Mary, king and queen of England'. Her later groat also includes Philip in the legend. (23 mm–30 mm.)

A range of smaller Elizabethan coins: halfpenny, penny, a milled threepence, groat and sixpence. In 1561 French moneyer Eloye Mestrell introduced the first screw press to the Tower Mint. This was powered in part by a horse-drawn mill (hence, milled coins). Although the output was superior to those hammered out by hand the process was slow and, probably more importantly, raised the ire of the traditional moneyers, and the experiment was abandoned. Mestrell was dismissed in 1572. In an ironic twist of fate he was hanged for counterfeiting six years later. (11 mm–25 mm.) (First two by permission of Wildwinds.com, third courtesy Museums Victoria)

James I to Charles I

With a family tree somewhat characteristic of royal dynasties, the lineage of the succeeding kings of England begins in Scotland with the marriage in 1315 of Marjorie Bruce, daughter of Robert the Bruce (1306–1329), to William Stewart, sixth High Steward of Scotland. Their male descendants ruled as kings of Scotland in an unbroken line to James V (1513–1542), who married Mary of Guise. Their daughter, also Mary, was crowned Queen of Scotland in 1542. She married into the French royal household in 1558, though her husband Francis died just two years later.

Margaret Tudor, daughter of England's Henry VII, married Archibald Douglas, Earl of Angus. Their daughter, also named Margaret, married another Stewart – Matthew. In 1545 their son Henry Stuart (or Stewart) was born, who is perhaps better remembered as Lord Darnley.

Mary, Queen of Scots married her second cousin, Lord Darnley, in 1565, though the marriage lasted only two years. Their child James was born in 1566. A year later an explosion destroyed Darnley's house and he was found, murdered, in the garden. Mary and her favourite, the Earl of Bothwell, were implicated in this event. She agreed to abdicate and fled to England. The infant James duly ascended to the throne of Scotland as James VI (1567–1625). After numerous intrigues and plots (real or concocted) Mary was beheaded at Fotheringhay Castle, Northamptonshire, in 1587 on the orders of another second cousin, Elizabeth I of England. Mary and Lord Darnley's son, James, was

Elizabeth's second cousin once removed, and being her closest male heir was crowned King James I of England in 1603.

Mary's coinage encompassed a range of issues that mirrored the main events of this period: in gold, silver and small change in billon, including placks and lions ('hardheads'), formed with very little silver. So many forgeries of placks and hardheads of Mary had appeared, particularly from Flanders and imported into Scotland, that placks dated 1557 were forbidden to circulate in 1572. It took until 1575 for both denominations to be inspected at the mint. Those deemed genuine were countermarked with a star within a heart and allowed back into circulation. Such a wholesale loss of small change must have caused considerable hardship to the majority of Scottish society for whom such currency was an essential feature of everyday life. To compound this problem, lower denomination Scottish issues often migrated south to the north of England, where they were welcomed as small change.

In England, mainstream issues of the now James I of England followed the universal trends of most precious metal coinages and by 1612 fluctuations in the price of bullion and a significant influx from abroad had provoked an economic crisis and subsequent revaluation of the coinage. The smallest change comprised silver halfpennies and pennies. No farthings were issued and everyday commerce was becoming increasingly difficult due to the lack of adequate smaller denominations. Sir Robert Cotton, MP and antiquarian, lobbied King James in 1611 for action on this concern when he reported that 'there were above three thousand retailers of victuals and small wares, in, and about London, that used their own tokens'. Public demands for centrally issued low-value coins were also becoming increasingly plaintive and persistent, especially in urban areas and where a wage-based economy was becoming dominant.

James had had experience in Scotland with small change not made wholly of precious metal and was not quite as averse as previous sovereigns to the concept of low-value base

Mary, Queen of Scots. The first coins are a billon plack dating to 1557, before her marriage to Francis; while the second, the billon lion of 1559, has the monogram 'FM' (Francis and Mary) as the obverse type. Both are countermarked with a star within a heart. The imposing silver ryal of 1566 – with the rather intriguing reverse design for a Scottish coin of a tortoise climbing a crowned palm tree – names herself and Henry, Lord Darnley. By 1578 the value of silver had risen considerably and silver coins were revalued and countermarked with a crowned thistle, as on the ryal. (15 mm–43 mm.)

metal issues. It might also have been in his mind that as he could not supress the practice of private tokens he may as well produce his own and make a profit from it. To this end James granted a licence to Lord Harington to issue tinned-copper farthings in 1613 – he, too, could see that a handsome profit could be made. Although the tinning imitated silver, they were small and unpopular coins and were soon withdrawn in favour of larger copper farthings. The obverse featured a crown and crossed sceptres while the reverse presented an Irish harp. Lord Harington died shortly after receiving the patent and his widow took over the operation. She sold it on to the Duke of Lennox, and on his death in 1624 it passed on to his widow, the Duchess of Richmond. These issues remained unpopular and were extensively forged – after all, four of them were worth one shiny silver penny – and this gave rise to the expression 'not worth a brass farthing'. As with near contemporary Spanish forgeries, the manufacture of some was laughably atrocious. In order to encourage their use twenty-one shillings worth were offered for twenty shillings worth of silver, but circulation remained uneven, with some areas handling very few and many people finding it difficult to exchange them for 'real' money. In retrospect the entire operation might have been better served had it been under the control of the Royal Mint, but James, notwithstanding his Scottish experience, could not agree to an official regal issue – an attitude adopted by his successors for decades to come.

The farthings continued to be issued by the Duchess of Richmond for Charles I (1625–1649) until 1634, when the lease was sold to Lord Maltravers. Two years later the Irish harp was replaced by a rose. Parliament took control of the production of these coins in 1643 and ended this operation a year later. A resolution was passed that all farthings should be redeemed from money raised from the estates of those who had issued them.

By then Charles had other matters to attend to and no doubt spared not a thought for small trifling base coins. His earlier lower denomination silver coinage had continued the traditions of his predecessors. With the outbreak of the Civil War in 1642 mints began

James I, halfpenny and penny, 1603–1604; halfpenny and penny, 1604–1619, with (English) rose and (Scottish) thistle. Larger denomination coins included for the first time in their legends reference to 'MAG.BRIT' (Magnae Britanniae – Great Britain). (11 mm–14 mm.) (Second courtesy Museums Victoria, others with permission of wildwinds.com.)

to operate in towns loyal to the king, from Carlisle in the north to Exeter and Truro in the south-west. Mints were also opened in Royalist towns under siege, such as Newark. In all, except Aberystwyth, the lowest denomination minted was the penny. The Royalist cause was not entirely forsaken when Charles was executed in 1649 but carried on in the name of Charles II until 1651; by then the Commonwealth had been issuing silver coins for two years, the smallest denomination being a somewhat diminutive halfpenny. With the uncertainty that came with living in a land at war with itself, coinage large and small was too precious to be abandoned to those who had no misgivings about taking it from you, with the inevitable result that it ebbed out of circulation and into spaces under floorboards and other hiding places.

Above: Farthings of James I, the first a Harington Type 2. (*c.* 16 mm.)

Below: Farthings of Charles I. The first two types were also authorised for use in Ireland. The middle specimen is a lamentable forgery. The rose tokens were also authorised for Ireland but do not appear to have left the mainland. (12 mm–16 mm.)

Charles I, silver penny, 1625–1642; halfpenny and groat of Aberystwyth (the only mint to produce halfpennies), 1638/9–1642; (9 mm–23 mm.) (First with permission of wildwinds. com, others courtesy Museums Victoria)

Apart from the halfpenny, Commonwealth issues (1649–1660) had a uniform pattern for all denominations and were nicknamed 'breeches money' due to the two shields of the reverse (representing St George's Cross and an Irish harp) appearing as a pair of seventeenth-century breeches – baggy trousers worn to the knee. Legends were in English rather than Latin so as to more truly represent Protestantism. Silver halfpenny, penny, halfgroat, sixpence. (9 mm–23 mm.) (Halfpenny and sixpence courtesy Museums Victoria)

Seventeenth-Century Tokens

Although lead tokens had been produced in greater numbers from 1644, towards the end of the decade a mere shortage of small change had progressed to becoming a severe dearth. This intolerable situation was soon to be relieved with an eruption of private and corporate copper tokens. In contrast to the lead and other tokens that had circulated since the Middle Ages, these prominently displayed details of their issuer, usually by name, location and trade along with the date of issue. Occupations were often displayed through the pictorial device of the arms of one of the guild companies of London; on other tokens representations of tools or similar symbols indicated the issuer's profession. As with pub and shop signs, this helped a largely illiterate population recognise the nature of the establishment – the devices on tokens identified the issuer.

This series offers a fascinating insight into Commonwealth and Restoration times as they were issued by many different types of trader, merchant and craftsman, and by enterprises such as mines, cockfighting, ferrymen, rodent officers, hospitals, tennis courts and prisons. They also highlight that women, far from being tied to the hearth and nursery, were actively involved in commerce and manufacture.

For centuries coining money had been a royal prerogative: after Charles I's execution this entitlement was no longer relevant and the first farthing tokens began to appear, gradually becoming more plentiful. Halfpenny tokens were subsequently issued, largely because the Commonwealth halfpenny had been demonetised, though it was also the case that a greater profit could be enjoyed by manufacturer and issuer from this higher denomination. Around 1660 it was believed that official issues would be forthcoming, and production slowed. The middle of the decade witnessed another escalation of token-issuing when these hopes were dashed, though within a couple of years it was again alleged that officialdom would relieve the situation and emissions slackened once more. Prosecutions of issuers and manufacturers at this time was another limiting factor, though royal pardons were later given. When a regal issue of farthings and halfpennies finally began in 1672, the tokens became redundant, though a few may have remained

The first, an undated farthing with the arms of the Merchant Guild of Bakers, was issued by William Osborne of Braintree, Essex, a town which Flemish immigrants made famous for its wool-cloth trade in the seventeenth century. The second, a 1663 halfpenny, is from James Cheever of Canterbury. The hand holding a pair of shears probably represents the wool trade. 'The Cros Shvfles' (crossed shovels) on the farthing of 1653 from Bow Street, Westminster, may be the sign of a maltster, making malt from cereal grain for use in breweries. As each ale-selling establishment brewed their own it may be assumed that the malt produced would find a ready market in the many nearby taverns and alehouses. Bow Street was laid out in the late 1630s, so HBS would have been an incomer to the newly built street. (16 mm–20 mm.)

in circulation at reduced values after this date. For the first twenty years only round tokens were struck, though around 1668 octagonal, heart-shaped and square tokens began to appear. These are all scarce and may owe more to their novelty value than to any pragmatism.

A very common place of issue across the country was in the many and varied alcohol-serving establishments. For centuries they had been places where 'gentlemen' could meet to discuss various matters over an ale or cider and put the world to rights. The Mermaid in London's Cheapside was made famous by William Shakespeare and his chums doing just that around 1600. In certain concerns, perhaps, some of the clientele might also attend to less salubrious matters and opportunities. The motives for landlords to issue tokens could thus be many and varied; for example, as change when a larger denomination coin was proffered and for prepayment of drink, food or services.

The profits made by these private issuers did not go unnoticed and town councils and other corporate bodies considered that they too should become involved in this undertaking. For example, on 24 March 1653 the Town Book for Northampton records that, 'Whereas there are diverse brasse halfpence dispersed abroad in this town by diverse persons ... It is ordered that the same shalbe all suppressed and that the Chamberlins of this town shall forthwth for the benifit of the poor disburse fortie shillings for farthin tokens to be stamped with the town arms upon them.' Many other towns, or through officers on its behalf, issued tokens, usually with some indication that they were for the 'poor's benefit' or for 'necessary change'. Were such pieces principally for the poor, and not of value to anyone making a small purchase? The stress on the destitute suggests that poverty in post-Civil War England was a major issue.

The halfpenny token of Abingdon, 1667, was issued by mercer Sarah Pleydell. Her husband-to-be, Samuel Pleydell, moved to Abingdon in 1633, shortly after receiving a legacy of £100 under his father's will. Here he set up in business as a grocer, and married local girl Sarah Stacey. In the Corporation chamberlain's accounts for 8 May 1645 an entry records that Samuel was paid £5 4s 1d for supplying ale at the request of the Corporation to Sir Thomas Fairfax's Parliamentary troops. Quite independently of any Abingdon ale drinking, the following month Fairfax's forces crushed the Royalists at Naseby, east of Rugby. Samuel died in 1663 and his wife Sarah continued the business. The sign on the obverse of the second halfpenny, 1667, shows what may be considered an unusual female occupation – that of an ironmonger. It is likely that Mary Brine of Barford, Warwickshire, also took over the business after her husband's death. Variations in spelling are visible on these two tokens: halfe/half and penny/peny. English spelling did not become standardised until long after this period. (19 mm, 21 mm.)

The first farthing here was issued by Valentine Hayward of 'The Mairmead Tavern at Billingate, 1650'. This Mermaid Tavern lay only a short walk from its more famous namesake in Cheapside. It was situated on the corner of Lower Thames Street and Pudding Lane, where the Great Fire of London began in 1666. The second undated farthing is from Humphrey Bodicott, vintner of Oxford. At the age of fifteen he began a nine-year apprenticeship in this trade. He ran his first tavern until 1636. These premises were recognised by an outside display of a simple vintner's bush (a sign, probably with Roman roots, showing a place where wine was sold). Three years later he took a lease on a tavern opposite All Souls College, which during his tenure appears to have become known as the Three Tuns (large casks), hence the reverse type. The obverse is a rendering of a vintner's bush, here with a wicker framework supporting grapes. Humphrey was elected Mayor of Oxford for 1647/8. It was the shortest mayoral term Oxford had ever witnessed: he was suspected of being a Royalist and was removed from office after only four days. Whatever side he supported, by 1649 he was providing wine to the value of £5 1s 8d for a banquet in honour of Sir Thomas Fairfax, the victor at Naseby. (15 mm.)

Towns and corporations. 'I.S in Northampton'. The initials are of John Stevens, one of the town's chamberlains in 1657–58 and 1658–59, the period when he issued this farthing token. The second, a farthing of Luke Nourse, Mayor of Gloucester in 1657, explicitly states its function: 'For necessary change'. Luke was heavily involved in the Parliamentary cause and during the siege of the city in 1643 was one of thirteen captains in the two Parliamentary regiments which lay in garrison. The town of Andover, Hampshire, began to issue a series of farthing tokens in 1658 which showed a cripple on the obverse. This image relates to the Poor Law, which was formalised in 1601. Their halfpenny token from 1666 makes this additionally clear with the inscription 'For Yᵉ Poores Benefit'. The reverse shows the town arms. The fourth is 'A Taunton Farthing/By the Constables, 1667'. The 'T' is overlain by a tun, which presumably contained West Country cider. The reverse displays the town gate. Finally, a very clear and austere message from Blandford Forum, Dorset: 'The Borough of Blandford, their Corporation/Farthing for the Use of Yᵉ Poore. 1669'. A note on 'Yᵉ'. The 'Y' is a legacy of Anglo-Saxon writing. This letter, known as 'thorn', is equivalent to 'th'. 'Yᵉ' in this sense therefore means (and should be pronounced) 'the'. On this token both spellings are used, 'The' and 'Yᵉ'. (15 mm–21 mm.)

Patterns and Milled Coinage

On a number of occasions during this period the prospect of government issues for small change was deliberated. In the cases when this was raised above the theoretical, patterns were struck for consideration by mints, government officials and royalty. These were often more attractive than any coinages arising from them, for at this later stage utility and cost become more significant.

The first experiment with milled coinage had been undertaken during the time of Elizabeth I, but it was not a success. Charles I employed Nicholas Briot, another Frenchman, to produce milled issues in 1632, though the Civil War intervened and this was abandoned. Patterns of milled coins were produced for Oliver Cromwell by Thomas Simon, using machinery provided by Peter Blondeau, but that came to naught with the restoration of the monarchy in 1660. Two years later Blondeau was recalled by Charles II (1660–1685) to produce England's first milled issues for general circulation. After nearly 2,000 years the era of hammered coinage production had ended.

Nevertheless, for all the patterns and worthwhile ambitions, it took until 1672 for small change to be issued in base metal. Henceforth, England and Britain could enjoy a set of milled coins in gold and in silver, and regally issued small change in base metal. Unfortunately, these agreeable intentions briskly faded before the dawn of the new century.

Patterns for small change. Elizabeth I, farthing in silver, 1601; Commonwealth period farthing; Charles II farthing, 1662; Charles II halfpenny, 1665 – with the success of this new design Britannia would once again grace the coins of England. (13.5 mm–32 mm.) (First with permission of wildwinds.com, others courtesy Museums Victoria)

Milled issues of Charles II: farthing 1674; halfpenny (here a proof issue, carefully struck from a special die with a mirror-like surface), 1672; so as to support the Cornish tin industry farthings were later produced in tin with a copper plug, as with this example from 1684; sixpence, 1683 (with engraved initials 'HG'). (20 mm–29 mm.) (Middle two courtesy Museums Victoria)

Coins, Coining Crimes and Harsh Punishments: 1686–1696

In the seventeenth century coining crimes were still dealt with most harshly. On 2 June 1686, for example, Alice Millikin was burnt at the stake at Smithfield for 'clipping the king's coin'. Felons found guilty of murder at the same hearing were merely hanged, as were men guilty of coining. The Proceedings of the Old Bailey show that 424 defendants were committed to trial for coining offences for the years 1686 to 1695, comprising over 10 per cent of the court's business. Perhaps surprisingly, over a half of those convicted were women, who then suffered the same fate as Alice Millikin. The crimes were offences against the monarch – high treason – and so attracted the severest penalties. By the 1690s the transgressions were a concern to central government and to some of England's prominent citizens, including Isaac Newton, warden and later master of the Royal Mint from 1696 to 1727. Their ubiquity was a major driving force behind the silver recoinage of 1696, and ostensibly inspired the foundation of the Bank of England in 1694.

The two main coining crimes were forging and clipping. The usual nature of forgeries is to produce a coin where the precious metal content is far lower than the original: for instance, silver-washing over a mould-cast base metal copy. However, forgeries require specialist skills and a far easier and more common crime was clipping. It has been estimated that in 1694 about two-thirds of hammered silver coins in circulation were extensively clipped. So as to combat this practice the Act for Preventing Counterfeiting and Clipping was passed in 1695. This Act allowed for a reward of £40 to those who apprehended and successfully prosecuted offenders – a staggering amount given that a labourer's wage was about a shilling a day.

The government decided to call in all hammered coins in 1696. Ill-advisedly, they made the astonishing mistake of accepting them, clipped or otherwise, at face value in exchange for the newly minted milled coins. Unsurprisingly this led to a great hoarding of the new coins and an escalation in the clipping of pre-1662 issues. The general public's reaction to this coin activity, legal or otherwise, was apparently a certain complacency. Bad coin would be passed on neighbour to neighbour and accepted at face value: after all, a coin is only as valuable as seller and buyer agree it is – which is likely to have made the activities of clippers and forgers easier to carry out, despite the penalties if they were caught.

1690s small change: William and Mary (1689–1694) fourpence, 1691; tin farthing with copper plug, 1690; copper farthing, 1694; William III (1694–1702), farthing, 1696. (17 mm, 22 mm.) (First two courtesy Museums Victoria)

Two hammered half-crowns of James I and Charles I. The first is an oddity. It probably started off as a forgery with a silver-washed copper core, imitating a genuine full-weight issue. In this scenario it must have fooled someone as it was subsequently clipped. However, it could have been manufactured as a clipped coin, following the trend of most of the genuine coins in circulation such as the half-crown of Charles I which had all its legend removed. Originally this coin measured around 35 mm across, but now only 23 mm remains. (21 mm–23 mm.) (First courtesy Museums Victoria)

From Queen Anne to the Late Eighteenth Century

The eighteenth century began as the seventeenth had ended, with insufficient small change being issued by regal authority. This longstanding tradition would continue throughout the century. During the reign of Queen Anne (1702–1714) no copper coinage was issued – though a pattern farthing was produced for 1714 and a few of these escaped into circulation. The lowest denomination minted was a small silver penny. Thereafter the copper series, following types initiated under Charles II, were not issued consistently, nor to any great extent, and lightweight forgeries began to fill the requirement for small money. Other ways of dealing with this problem emerged in the last quarter of the century when those for whom everyday coinage was essential took matters into their own hands. This, too, was now a British habit, one with a pedigree stretching back approximately seventeen centuries.

The 1700s witnessed Britannia ruling the waves and establishing an empire across the continents. At home the century began with an agricultural revolution and ended with Britain arising as the first industrialised nation. Times were changing in the fields of science, technology, religion, philosophy and political ideology, as well as in regard to how groups in society viewed each other. While at a surface level these simple statements have some validity, they mask the many underlying influences at work during (and before) the eighteenth century. They also tend to imply that the country entered the century as a wholly agrarian society and left it fully fledged as an industrial nation, one where everyone shared the benefits of these revolutions. Though agricultural production rose, and considerably so in certain regions, it did not do so uniformly across the country. Moreover, the first of the expanding industries were sited on or close to available mineral and fuel deposits, or on areas where water power could be exploited to drive cotton mill machinery, all of which by their nature are localised resources, and by and large much of the country carried on as before.

During the latter half of the century there was, however, a rapid growth in population and an increased drift from countryside to urban and industrial areas. Many of these were new creations on greenfield sites: for example, Merthyr Tydfil was a small insignificant farming community at the end of a south Wales valley before ironworks at Dowlais and Cyfarthfa were established in 1767 – by the 1830s Dowlais Ironworks was the largest in the world, employing more than 5,000 people. In tandem with these developments arose, on one hand, the growth of philanthropy, often founded on Christian principles, and on the other a certain disdain directed at the 'proletariat' – not least in the expression by politician and philosopher James Burke in 1790, who described them as 'the swinish multitude'. Difficulties in application of the Poor Law were becoming increasingly apparent, for which the responses varied from parish to parish. Throughout all this, and with an expansion in the proportion of wage earners, one factor remained constant: cash was becoming increasingly paramount, especially everyday coinage – of which there was still very little.

The first of the inevitable lightweight forgeries began to appear by the half-century mark. In 1753 it was reckoned that a half or more of copper money was irregular; by the 1780s Matthew Boulton was reporting that two-thirds of the change he received passing through tollgates between London and Birmingham was made up of forged coins. With the death penalty remaining available for those found guilty of forging coins of the realm a new approach was taken. So as to evade the law's harsh penalties halfpennies were produced which imitated regal issues but had nonsensical legends that were made up of approximately the same number of letters as official coins. People who could not read presumably passed them on innocently, while those who were literate probably did not care about the coin's origin (so long as it could be passed on to the next person), as the well-worn state of the illustrated examples testify. The production of these 'evasives' petered out when the venerated British practice of private tokens began anew.

Eighteenth-century smaller denominations: sixpence of Queen Anne, 1711; 'Dump' halfpenny of George I, 1717; George II halfpenny, 1736, and sixpence, 1757; George III, threepence, 1762. (17 mm–28 mm.)

Continuity in the design of infrequently issued regal farthings: George I (1714–1727), 1719; George II (1727–1760), 1730 and 1746; George III (1760–1820), 1773. (22 mm.)

Lightweight cast forgeries that spent much time in circulation. The first appears to be an exceptionally thin forgery of a farthing, though it could have started life as a gaming counter. The second, dated '1773', shows a characteristic flaw of a crude casting process: bubbles on the surface. The well-worn '1772' halfpenny emerged from the mould slightly warped; the other with unclear date (probably 1773) shows other casting flaws, particularly at ten o'clock on the reverse. All have the distinctive 'soapy' feel of cast copies. (20 mm–28 mm.)

Evasive halfpennies. The legend on the first, with the bust of George II, reads 'George Rules', while the second with the bust of George III reads 'Claudius Romanus'. The reverse inscriptions are 'North Wales' (with harp) and 'Delectas Rus' – 'The Country Delights'. What are probably later issues diverge from this theme and include other personages, including King Alfred with a modified Britannia reverse and the legend 'Briton's Glory', the latter word at the bottom, in the exergue. The obverse showing Sir Bevois, the mythical founder of Southampton, is a copy of tokens issued in that town in 1791. The reverse shows a harp and 'North Wales'. This is a hybrid creation, a 'mule', as the obverse and reverse dies were not originally meant to be used together. (c. 28 mm.)

Regal coins can be found bearing countermarks, though it is usually impossible to date them to either this or a later period. The first two here are a much-worn Charles II farthing with an axe (?) countermark and an equally threadbare George II halfpenny countermarked 'I.A'. Two George III halfpennies, 1772 and 1773, the first countermarked 'RI', the second 'TS' on the obverse, with a pair of scissors on the reverse. Was TS a barber, a tailor, or something quite different, such as a utensil sharpener? (22 mm–28 mm.)

Late Eighteenth-Century Tokens

The first British tokens of the late eighteenth century were pennies issued in 1787 by the copper mine at Parys Mountain on the island of Anglesey. With no small change available the employer was forced to pay wages to a group of men with silver coins or, much less often, a note. The men (or their wives, if they were married) then had to spend this collectively in whatever store they chose to visit. This unsatisfactory arrangement in a sparsely populated area with few retail outlets gave impetus to the issue of the penny, and later a halfpenny. John Wilkinson, ironmaster and builder of the first iron bridge, quickly did likewise, issuing his own ample series beginning the same year. The floodgates had been opened and across the country others followed.

Although initially manufactured by industrialists and traders to solve the problem of a lack of everyday coinage, the emission of these tokens was more complex than that of seventeenth-century issues. Those that were clearly commercial small change had impressed around the edge a formula such as 'Payable in London and Birmingham' or 'Payable by I. Gibbs Lamberhurst' – that is, places where they were redeemable for coin of the realm. Some, such as the so-called 'National Series' or those issued by counties or by anyone willing to purchase tokens from the Birmingham makers and which were issued anonymously, occasionally had 'Payable in Somewhere', but often no place of repayment was stated. As with most tokens, there were many occasions when it proved impossible to redeem a certain issue, and those who bore the subsequent loss were consumers at the bottom of the chain, those left holding worthless 'money'. As beneficial as the tokens were for generating small change, their informal nature (and misapplication) could lead to public disapproval.

Some tokens were produced simply for advertisement purposes, or to act as shop tickets, and yet others to carry a political or social message. It was soon realised that all these tokens had a certain charm and better-quality examples were produced for the collecting market. Countermarking also became commonplace – a cheap and no-risk alternative for those unable or unwilling to issue their own tokens. Finally, as harsh penalties did not apply to these private releases, many lightweight forgeries appeared.

Anglesey penny, 1787, and halfpenny, 1791, with a druid's head and the cypher 'PMCo' for Parys Mine Company. The legend states 'We Promise to Pay the Bearer One Penny', with the edge inscription 'On Demand in London Liverpool or Anglesey'. The halfpenny's reverse legend is 'The Paris Miners Halfpenny', while the edge states 'Payable at Birmingham London or Bristol'. Although this piece is full weight and appears to have been struck from genuine dies, the legend exposes it as a forgery. It may have been manufactured by an errant individual, although there is another possible explanation: it could have been struck by a wayward workman for selling to collectors at a high price. All the Anglesey issues were considerably forged. The 1794 halfpenny from Winchelsea, Sussex, was issued by Richard Maplesden, grocer and draper. The reverse arms are those of the port of Sandwich. The obverse, with the legend 'Industry, the Source of Content', shows a bee hive (strictly speaking, a skep) with industrious worker bees swarming around, a small shrub to the left and an overhanging seed-bearing rose bush on the right – a metaphor for the rise of industrial capitalism? (33 mm–29 mm.)

A change of emphasis. Whereas seventeenth-century tokens often proclaimed they were for 'the poor's benefit', late eighteenth-century issues had broader ambitions as shown in these legends: 'For Change Not Fraud', I. Gibbs, Lamberhurst, Kent/Sussex, 1794; 'For the Use of Trade', struck for three traders, Samuel Prentice, grocer and chandler, Samuel Delf, whitesmith and brazier, and Matthias Abel, grocer and draper, all in Bungay, Suffolk, 1795; 'For the Convenience of Society', John Foller, Northam, Sussex, 1794; 'For the Public Good', G. Ring, Frant, Sussex, 1794. (c. 28 mm.)

Industry and infrastructure. The first coin, from John Wilkinson for his ironworks in Warwickshire, 1791, features Vulcan, the Roman god of fire and metalworking. With the setting up of the first turnpike road in 1663 roads were maintained by a trust who charged a toll for those travelling along them. The number of such roads increased during the eighteenth century. A mail coach with the legend 'Mail Coach Halfpenny Payable in London' adorns the halfpenny from Middlesex, while the reverse reads 'To J. Palmer Esq This is Inscribed as a Token of Gratitude for Benefits Rece.d from the Establishment of Mail Coaches'. However, this was to become the age of the canal. The obverse of the next, 1792, has a sailing barge passing under the first cast-iron bridge, erected in 1779 at Coalbrook-Dale, Shropshire. The reverse shows an engineering marvel, the inclined plane at Ketley which could lift a laden boat 66 feet. It was issued by Reynolds & Co., who cast the bridge. The issue from Brinscombe Port, Gloucester, 1795, has a Severn trow (a sailing barge) with the legend 'Thames and Severn Canal'. The reverse displays the entrance to Sapperton Tunnel, an engineering triumph of its day at 2½ miles long. (c. 28 mm.)

Traders. Niblock & Hunter, 'General Commission & Public Saleroom', Bridge Street, Bristol, 1795, with Justice and a lion above a packing case. Richard Paley, maltster, soap boiler and chandler, Leeds, depicting Bishop Blaze and the town arms of Leeds, 1791. John Fielding, grocer and tea dealer, Manchester, 'East India House' and the crest of the Grocers' Company, 1792. (c. 28 mm.)

Anonymous issues. The first two from Middlesex, 1795, portraying George, Prince of Wales, with his badge on the reverse. The former, with the reverse legend 'Industry is the Parent of Success', has an edge reading 'Payable in Lancaster London or Bristol', the second, with star countermark, 'Payable at Dublin Cork or Belfast'. The third, showing Sir Isaac Newton, Middlesex, 1793, reads 'Payable in London Bristol Lancaster'. (c. 28 mm.)

Tradesmen's tickets. John Jelly, Botanic Gardens, Bath, Somerset, 1794, presumably illustrating areas of the garden, with religious inscriptions: 'He Spake of Trees, from the Cedar Tree that is in Lebanon'; 'Even unto the Hyssop that Springeth out of the Wall', in the exergue 'I:Kings:Ch:4.V:33'. A year after this token was issued Mr Jelly was declared bankrupt and items from the botanic gardens were sold off. Salter & Co. moved the 'Cheapest Hat Warehouse in the World' to No. 47 Charing Cross, London, in 1793. Their token shows the interior of a hatter's shop with workers engaged in various tasks. The reverse shows the front of a typical eighteenth-century shop. (c. 28 mm.)

Although the first tokens of the eighteenth century were struck for a Welsh mine, the country as a whole – as with some northern areas of England – did not require a considerable token coinage. The first three here are anonymous farthings: 'North Wales', 'South Wales', and a 'Medallion of Saint David', all dated 1793, with 'Pro Bono Publico' – 'For the Good of the Public'. The latter token can be found listed under Britain's smallest city, St David's in Pembrokeshire, but the lack of any possessive tells that it is a generic Welsh issue commemorating the country's patron saint. The halfpenny token of 1795 is the sole example bearing legends in the Welsh language: 'Jestyn ap Gwrgan Tywysog Morganwg 1091' – 'Jestyn, son of Morgan, Prince of Glamorgan', and 'Y Brenhin ar Grfraith' – the last word is in error and should read 'Cyfraith' – 'The King by Law'. The obverse shows King Jestyn, the reverse, Britannia. It was struck by Jorden, a token manufacturer in Birmingham, apparently for his father. Its area of circulation is unknown. (*c.* 20 mm, 28 mm.)

Political and social issues. Across the Channel in France ferment had mushroomed into revolution by 1789, a situation of some concern for the elites in the rest of Europe. Thomas Spence (1750–1814), a coin dealer, was a leading English radical of the late eighteenth century. Originally from Newcastle, he moved to London in 1792, from where he issued a large number of politically inspired tokens which promoted ideas such as an end to aristocracy and for all land to be publically owned by self-governing 'democratic parishes' – dangerous thoughts indeed. He also published many pamphlets, including *Property in Land Every One's Right* in 1775, later re-issued as *The Real Rights of Man*, and the penny periodical *Pig's Meat* – a reference to Burke's vicious description of the English masses. The first of two tokens of Spence exhibits a man on a gibbet with the legend 'The End of Pain'. The reverse legend 'May the Knave of Jacobin Clubs Never Get a Trick' is a reference to the Jacobin Club of France, led by Robespierre. The countermarked piece endorses 'Land in Partnership' 'And Every Blessing'. Spence spent six months in prison in 1784 for his endeavours, and twelve months in 1801 for seditious libel in connection with his pamphlet *The Restorer of Society to its Natural State*. The third token, showing Newgate Prison, 1794, bears the satirical legend 'Payable at the Residence of Messrs Symonds, Winterbotham, Ridgway & Holt'; they were incarcerated in this notorious gaol for sedition in 1794. The fourth is a commercial token issued in 1794 by William Gye, bookseller, printer and stationer in Bath. He was also agent to the Ilchester debtors and visited the jail weekly. In his shop he drew attention to the legend on his token – 'Remember the Debtors in Ilchester Goal' (the last word an unfortunate misspelling) – and kept a container on his counter for donations for the prisoners. In this period it was common practice for people to be sent to prison for even very small debts they could not repay; they could be imprisoned for life if they were unable to do so. The obverse shows Benevolence directing her key-carrying messenger to open a prison, the reverse the arms of the city of Bath. (25 mm–29 mm.)

Lightweight irregularities. The first halfpenny is a mule, with the standard obverse for John Wilkinson, and the reverse an obverse of a piece made by prolific token manufacturer Lutwyche of Birmingham showing Justice, with legend 'Medals & Provincial Coins' and 'Dea Pecunia' in the exergue. The following are likely to be forgeries, firstly of John Wilkinson's issue of a worker in a smithy, 1793, the second of John Voss, linen draper and mercer, with Swansea Castle and key, 1796, both with their edges 'bashed in', thereby obliterating any location telling where the originals would have been redeemable. (25 mm–28 mm.)

There was an additional problem which made certain types unpopular: the 'truck system'. With poor road networks and no shops in some of the more remote places, owners and employers of industrial concerns paid wages with distinctive tokens which could only be spent in their shop. This regrettably led to higher prices being charged than would have been the case in regular stores. Although this meant that the employers could offset the wages paid to attract workers it was an unscrupulous system which defrauded those who had no choice. A number of bills were presented to Parliament to halt this activity; however, it took until 1887 for the truck system to finally discontinue and for workers in all locations to be paid in coin of the realm.

Countermarking, sporadically practiced in the early part of the century, began to intensify towards its end, appearing first on early regal issues then on tokens. Anglesey halfpenny, 1789, countermarked for 'E-A'. The 'RS' countermark was applied to a halfpenny of the Birmingham Mining & Copper Company, 1794, with Commerce seated and a stork perched on a cornucopia. The farthing, a county issue from Cambridgeshire, 1795, countermarked 'M', has the reverse legend 'Industry Has Its Sure Reward', a beehive and a swarm surrounding it – the growing metaphor for a new world order (whatever the truth regarding working conditions). The obverse shows a druid's head. (20 mm–29 mm.)

George III from 1797 to 1816

Wars in Europe stifled imports of Spanish-American silver and few coins in this metal were struck in the closing decades of the century. A lull in hostilities allowed for a drop in bullion prices and sixpences and shillings were minted in 1787, but prices rose steeply and production ceased. With no copper coinage struck after 1775 small denomination British coins had again reached rock bottom. In a miserable attempt to issue silver coinages, Spanish four and eight reales were counterstamped with the bust of the king and passed current as dollars (4s 9d) and half-dollars. This unsatisfactory situation was slightly alleviated in 1804 when Spanish eight reales were overstruck by the Bank of England and released as dollars with a face value of 5s until 1811, then at 5s 6d until withdrawn from circulation in 1817. In 1811 the bank issued silver coins worth 3s and 1s 6d. However, it is a telling sign of these times that their face value was greater than their silver content. They were issued openly as tokens.

Matthew Boulton (1728–1809) exemplifies a type of entrepreneurism arising during this period. He managed his father's hardware business in Birmingham until 1762, the year he built his nearby Soho manufactory, producing small items such as silver buttons and buckles. Six years later he made the acquaintance of James Watt as the need for a power source for his factory attracted him to Watt's invention, the steam engine, which had been patented in 1769 in partnership with industrialist John Roebuck. When Roebuck was declared bankrupt Boulton accepted his share as debt repayment. By 1775 Boulton and Watt had become partners in the steam engine business and the success achieved from erecting pumping engines to drain the Cornish tin mines established the viability and value of the new technology. Boulton turned his hand to applying steam technology to coin production in 1786, obtaining a patent in 1790, through which he minted large quantities of coins, including for the East India Company, and supplied machinery to the Royal Mint in London. He also manufactured a number of late eighteenth-century tokens for tradesmen and industrialists around the country.

For a brief time at the end of the eighteenth century an attempt was made to rectify the gross inadequacy of Britain's copper coinage and to suppress the use of tokens which had been widespread since 1787. Boulton was given a contract to supply regal copper coins. These emerged in 1797 as the first official pennies and twopences to appear in Britain minted in copper – namely, the celebrated 'cartwheels'. They contained their face value of metal and weighed in at 1 and 2 ounces respectively. The twopence was a particularly massive thing and no further issues were produced. When the price of copper rose the coins were worth more than their face value and many were melted down, exacerbating the shortage they had been meant to alleviate. The next issue of halfpence and farthings surfaced in 1799 – at a lower relative weight than coins of 1797, provoking the suspicion among the general public that they were being cheated.

'Cartwheel' penny, 1797; halfpenny and farthing, 1799; penny, 1807; and a grotesque cast copy of an 1806 halfpenny. (23 mm–35 mm.)

A Bank of England dollar overstruck from 1804 to 1811 by Boulton, all bearing the date 1804, on a Spanish eight reales, some 3 million of which had been 'captured' that year. At ten o'clock on the reverse 'HI' shows through – the first two letters of HISPANIA (Spain). With a rise in the price of silver many of these were melted down. The next is a genuine (and well-used) silver bank token for one shilling and sixpence, while the latter two are silver-washed forgeries of the three shilling token. The first has the silver-washing firmly embedded into the copper core, though this has worn away on the highest points – exposing its passage through many hands. The second, with only a brass core remaining, has been square-holed, presumably to highlight its true status. (27 mm–40 mm.)

A further issue of pennies, halfpence and farthings appeared in 1806/7. And that was that for the funding of an increasingly urban and industrialised nation, the world leader in this enterprise.

Tokens, 1811 to 1850

The examples produced by the Bank of England were not the only tokens to appear in 1811. Since the beginning of the century regal coinages, tokens and a motley collection of forgeries had been countermarked by those short of everyday small change. As time progressed these proved to be inadequate for more general use so, as always, the public took matters into their own hands. Copper token pennies, halfpennies and farthings were struck by traders and industrial concerns, and, for the first time, silver tokens also. Over the decades the cost of living had risen, and silver tokens were principally used to pay wages. The government did nothing to thwart this practice until it became clear that the ever-present ne'er-do-wells were refusing to redeem them and an Act in 1817 declared them illegal. The exception to this were workhouse tokens as it was understood that the unfortunates occupying these establishments could not endure losing the small value of money they had. These tokens were made illegal by 1823.

A collection of 'utilitarian' countermarks on regal coinage, the second on an 1811 halfpenny token of Walthamstow, Essex. As with many countermarks their date and place of application is unknown, and some of these may have been produced sometime later. However, they illustrate the type of material passing as small change during this period. (22 mm–33 mm.)

Crown countermarks on various pennies of George III. It was common practice from the late eighteenth century to incorporate a crown in brand or trademarks. This was particularly common in the metal trades, especially in Sheffield. (33 mm–36 mm.)

The 1811 penny token issued by the Rose Copper Company of Birmingham & Swansea bears a countermark of oak leaves and an acorn. The Carmarthen penny of 1812 illustrating the arms of Carmarthen and a cask within an oak wreath was issued by William Griffiths, an ironmonger with outlets in Carmarthen and Swansea. Tobacconists commonly dispensed tokens in both the seventeenth and eighteenth centuries, a trend which continued into the nineteenth century, such as this farthing of 1814 by John Elliot of Quayside, Newcastle, who dealt in 'Genuine Tobacco & Snuff' – the weed is prominently displayed. As tobacco was sold loose and by weight, were these tokens given out to round up the value of a quantity of tobacco, to be redeemed with the next purchase? (22 mm–33 mm.)

Publicising pride and innovations. John Williams of Scorrier House, Redruth, issued this Cornish penny in 1811. It shows a Newcomen pumping engine and the three principal products of the county: tin, fish and copper. Flint lead works offered 'One Pound Note for Every 240 Tokens' in 1813 and recorded the works with all chimneys bellowing out smoke. Bristol had been second only to London as a trading port from the Middle Ages onwards. The 1811 farthing token of 'Patent Sheathing Nail Manufactory' portrays a contemporary sailing vessel. (22 mm–33 mm.)

This silver sixpence token, with a castle surrounded by lions from 1811, was of Rushbury &
Woolley, military ornament manufacturers in Bilston, Staffordshire. Haverfordwest in
Pembrokeshire was a thriving little inland port on the western Cleddau, upstream from
Milford Haven, and the hub of the county. From 1811 the issuers of this shilling – Thomas &
Phillips, David Jardine, John Lloyd, and W&J Phillips – are believed to have been merchants
who probably occupied large and imposing warehouses on the quay. The town also boasts an
impressive castle, though not quite as illustrated on the token. The coming of the railway in
1853 devastated maritime and river traffic. Murfin & Parker, the issuers of the shilling token
of 1812, were drapers in Doncaster. (20 mm–26 mm.)

The dreaded workhouse. With a view of the workhouse itself, this 1813 penny token of the Sheffield Overseers of the Poor was subsequently countermarked neatly by 'Andrew'. Tokens of the Union Copper Company of Birmingham stated on their 1812 pennies that they were issued 'For Public Accommodation' – these tokens were often countermarked by both Bradford and Keighley workhouses. The Tunstead and Happing, Norfolk, halfpenny of 1812 was produced for the workhouse at Smallburgh. (30 mm–36 mm.)

The 'cartwheels' from 1797 were a favoured medium for countermarking during the early decades of the nineteenth century. Occasionally some are particularly intriguing. The first penny exhibits two crossed clay pipes which may have been the mark of either a pipe manufacturer or a tobacconist. The twopence has been punchmarked 'STEAM MILL', which presumably meant something to those working in one. The third, a penny, shows a diamond registration mark used to demonstrate when an item was first registered (rather like copyright). These were applied to items between 1842 and 1883. Here the mark records registration for a metal product on 2 November 1843. This could be a trial piece, assessing whether the punch was adequate for purpose before being applied to the item in question. The fourth, also a penny, may suggest that a 'Mr Crosland, Joseph' thought himself a 'Goody Peny', or that his penny was good (for example, he would behave honestly) and advertised the fact. However, it might carry a political message. Joseph Crosland led his family's textile firm in Huddersfield and served as Conservative Member of Parliament for the town from 1893 to 1895, though he had contested the previous three elections and lost. He was knighted in 1889, thus this endorsement could have been connected with one of his unsuccessful attempts to become an MP before he was knighted. (36 mm–40 mm.)

King George III, from 1816, to Queen Victoria, 1860

Modernity finally came to the Royal Mint in 1816 when it moved from its ancient and inadequate premises in the Tower of London to its new site on Tower Hill, where steam-powered machinery had been installed by Boulton and Watt. Its first task was to begin a complete recoinage – in gold and (slightly lightweight) silver, though copper coins were ignored. These were the first of a coinage which was to remain legal tender until decimalisation. The half-crowns were unflatteringly known as 'bull heads'.

The silver coinage for George IV (1820–1830) was struck with a number of reverse types over this short rule. On the obverse, the first bust portraying the king was disliked by the monarch; it was changed to something more to his taste in 1825. Farthings were issued the year after George's coronation, though it took until 1825 for copper pennies and halfpennies to be struck. All three denominations showed the seated Britannia reverse, a type first employed by Charles II, though now Britannia is seated facing right. This tradition was followed by his younger brother, William IV (1830–1837), although, again, copper coins were not struck every year. During this reign slavery was abolished and the Reform Act was introduced which redistributed parliamentary seats in line with the rapidly growing industrial towns and cities, replacing those constituencies in decaying areas which were often controlled by a single landowner who demanded (coerced, bullied) few voters to 'act accordingly' – the 'rotten boroughs'. The Act laid the foundations for a broader parliamentary democracy. Notwithstanding these developments, Dorset's Tolpuddle Martyrs were sentenced to transportation for daring to form a Friendly Society and the Corn Laws, though they protected the farmer, worked against the importation of cheaper cereals. Thus the price of bread remained high, a cost borne more demonstrably by the working classes and those beneath them.

In many countries of Europe, Princess Alexandrina Victoria would never have become queen. Her uncle, Ernest Augustus, Duke of Cumberland, was the eighth child and fifth son of George III and under the Salic law of Germany – which barred succession to a female – could have become king. However, the British system of male-preference primogeniture destined Victoria, the daughter of George's fourth son, Prince Edward, Duke of Kent, to be crowned queen in 1837. Ernest left Britain, where he was unpopular for his antipathy towards parliamentary reform, to become king of Hanover, the royal house which had ruled Britain since George I. British humour being what it is, it was not very long before satirical brass counters were produced which copied Victorian half sovereigns, where St George of the reverse was substituted by Ernest riding a horse, and the legend became 'To Hanover'.

The first coinage of Victoria's long reign carried on the system of her two uncles. In silver modifications to reverse designs were made; in copper there was little change. By 1849 decimalisation was being seriously considered so as to bring Britain in line with almost every other nation. To this end a new coin, the two shilling or florin, one-tenth of a pound, was produced that year. Oddly, D. G. – Dei Gratia, By the Grace of God – which normally followed after the monarch's name, was omitted from the legend.

George III. An 1816 'bull head' half-crown (a denomination colloquially known as a half-dollar), and a shilling (a bob) from 1817. The last three are a continuation of longstanding trends. An obverse of a shilling from 1816 countermarked with a crown and one from 1817 severely bashed with 'M'. The brass core of a silver-washed 1819 'shilling' has some silvering remaining. With rising prices the number of forged copper coins largely came to an end and criminals focussed on gold and silver issues. (23 mm–28 mm.)

These 'Godless' florins were quickly replaced with a new type, the 'Gothic' issue, which employed an archaic form of lettering with the date given in Latin numerals. Both of these show the queen wearing a crown. On all other denominations she is presented with her hair tied back, a representation not fundamentally altered until 1887.

From 1838, with the development of industry and urbanisation now at full speed, and with the British Empire continuing to expand, copper small change was finally issued annually, and in quantity. It had only taken nearly 2,000 years for the country to achieve this milestone.

George IV farthing, 1825, with first and disliked bust; shilling, 1826, with the more popular second. William IV four pence (groat), 1836, rendering a seated Britannia (the only British silver coin type to do so), known by the nickname of 'Joey', after Joseph Hume, who suggested the type. In later times this expression referred to threepences. The last three coins are a farthing, 1837; sixpence, 1835, countermarked 'W.F' in oval; and farthing, 1836, countermarked 'D'. (11 mm–23 mm.)

The first gold-looking brass counter satirises Prince (later King) Ernest, 'To Hanover', whence he departed with the blessing of the British public. The next was a commonly produced gaming counter of the eighteenth century, a copy of a Queen Anne sixpence. The worn state of this example might suggest it also saw service as currency. The next three are brass imitations of half and full 'spade' guineas (so named for the shape of the shield on the reverse) of George III. There are conflicting theories as to how these originated, though it is generally accepted that the first issues were gaming counters. They were also popular as props in the theatre and as an advertising medium. The series continued to be produced into the twentieth century. The first, a standard 'In Memory of the Good Old Days', was perhaps fabricated as late as the 1870s. The second is an advertising piece for John Wood and Joseph Rollason, diesinkers, tool makers, stampers and piercers, from *c.* 1873 to 1891, trading at No. 52 Tenby Street North, Birmingham. As with many of these pieces, it has been holed for use in jewellery – bling is nothing new. The final example was handed out to customers of J. Sainsbury, probably in connection with the opening of a new branch at Haymarket, Norwich, in 1913. (20 mm–25 mm.)

Queen Victoria (1837–1901): sixpence (a tanner), 1858; a 'Godless' 1849 florin; halfpenny and farthing, 1858; a ghastly lead/pewter forgery of a 'Gothic' florin dated MDCCCLXXII – 1872. (20 mm–30 mm.)

Queen Victoria from 1860 to Queen Elizabeth II

The general course of British silver coinage was established in the latter years of George III's reign, and remained so – with some exceptions and novel reverse designs – up to 1920. After the First World War, with wartime costs to be borne and a severe rise in the price of silver, the longstanding standard for silver coinage, .925, dropped to .500, though the types were not specifically modified. Following the next global conflict bullion was required to repay the loan made during the war years by the USA and silver coinage disappeared in 1947, being replaced by cupro-nickel. Again these followed the designs of their immediate predecessors. With no gold denominations forthcoming, Britain's money was now entirely made up of token issues.

By the late 1850s the relatively large copper coins of farthing, halfpenny and penny were considered too heavy and unwieldy for everyday use; they also wore quite quickly. At this time Australia was Britain's primary source for this metal, so when the Australian miners diverted their attention towards the fortunes to be made in the gold rush the price of copper rose. These factors resulted in the decision to abandon pure copper coinage and produce low denomination coins in bronze (a copper/tin alloy). These were more hardwearing than copper, lighter and cheaper to produce. The first issues were placed into circulation in December 1860. These coins continued to bear a seated Britannia reverse; in size and composition they closely resembled the bronze coins of France that had emerged in the early 1850s.

There were some changes to the currency prior to decimalisation. For example, the silver threepence was phased out by 1941, being replaced by a twelve-sided brass coin which had been proposed under Edward VIII (1936) but with his abdication was not released (although a few did escape into circulation). The new design featuring a thrift (also known as a sea-pink) began to be issued in 1937. When Elizabeth II ascended the throne the reverse type became a portcullis, a detail found on coins of Elizabeth I.

For those monarchs who ruled for a number of decades, minor modifications, and sometimes outright changes, can be observed in the style of the bust. On her silver coins, such as the shilling and half-crown, the bust of Queen Victoria changed little from her coronation up to the year of her Golden Jubilee (1887), when she was portrayed crowned. Her profile changed again in 1895 when she was shown veiled: the 'Widow's Head' coinage. Bronze coins from 1860 became known as 'Bun Head' issues due to the arrangement of her hair, which was tied behind her head. This type of bust remained in service, with subtle differences to age her portrait, until 1895, when it was replaced by the veiled 'Widow's Head'.

This system of coinage served Britain well for over a hundred years: a circulating currency with a full range of denominations, excepting gold coinage, which had transformed into Bank of England banknotes during the time of George V. In the 1960s it began to be seen as a little archaic and, for visitors to the country, rather arcane, so a scheme for issuing a new decimal currency system was deliberated. At this time the mint on Tower Hill was struggling to keep up with demand for both British coins and with contracts for nations overseas. In the spirit of decentralisation the decision was made in 1964 to transfer mint operations to Llantrisant in south Wales: the first phase opened in December 1968. After a transitional period the mint at Tower Hill ceased to produce coins in 1975. During these years Britain had become one of the last nations to adopt decimal coinage. The shilling and florin were issued as 'Five New Pence' and

'Ten New Pence' in 1968 in readiness for the day when Britain's historic currency was demonetised. The full set of decimal denominations became the country's coined money on 15 February 1971. A numismatic tradition had ended, though some of the iconic designs from previous centuries were adopted for the new money. The development of this coinage continues apace, as it makes its own history.

Shilling of Queen Victoria with a portrayal only slightly and occasionally revised on silver issues until 1887, when the crowned Jubilee Head was introduced. The 'Bun Head' bronze coinage was not radically altered up to the time of the veiled 'Widow's Head' of 1895, and here we have two farthings from 1887 and 1901. From 1897 to 1917 this denomination was artificially darkened to avoid confusion with gold half-sovereigns. For the duration of £ s d releases one profile bust represented Queen Elizabeth II. There was, however, one change. The first, a penny of 1953, includes as part of the obverse legend 'BRITT:OMN:REGINA', 'Queen of all the British Territories'. This formula (which began on coins of Edward VII ('BRITT:OMN:REX') was dropped the following year, as shown here on the halfpenny and sixpence. The legends on these translate as 'Elizabeth II, by the Grace of God, Queen, Defender of the Faith'. (20 mm–30 mm.)

Edward VII as shown on the obverse of this 1902 farthing, and throughout his reign. George V sixpences from 1912, and slightly modified, 1926. A difference in the rendering of George VI is shown on his halfpenny, from 1942, and two shillings of 1948. The 1950 penny to the right omits a certain category of royal titles: IND:IMP ('Indiae Imperator') – 'Emperor of India'. This epithet was first used on British coins in 1895 by the Empress of India, Queen Victoria. After India had attained independence in 1949 it was no longer applicable. (20 mm–30 mm.)

Some changes to reverse types were slight, others were more dramatic. From 1860 bronze coinage had depicted Britannia with a lighthouse to the left and a sailing ship on the right. From 1895 these were omitted and the newer version was used up to 1937 when, with a drastic break from tradition, Britannia was replaced by an alert wren. These farthings were last issued in 1956 and demonetised in 1961. Halfpennies broke with an almost 300-year ancestry at the same time, when the *Golden Hind* became the reverse type. Silver threepences had served since the time of William and Mary with a crowned numeral 3 prominently displayed, a type standardised under George IV. The issues from 1927 broke with this custom and oak leaves bearing three acorns became the reverse illustration. Under George VI this was changed to a shield on a rose. These were phased out when probably the foremost alteration to Britain's contemporary currency was introduced in 1937: the brass twelve-sided threepence. (16 mm–26 mm.)

These shillings exemplify both tradition and innovation in British currency over this period. Top left is the regular type up to 1887, when it was replaced with the royal arms. This in turn was supplanted in 1895 with three individual shields within a garter. The 1906 shilling of Edward VII harks back to a design first employed for George IV. It was also the basic emblem on shillings of George V. Under George VI and Elizabeth II a novel approach was taken. Two types of this denomination were placed into circulation simultaneously, one with an 'English' reverse (on the left), the other a 'Scottish' reverse. (23 mm.)

The firm of Ralph Heaton & Sons in Birmingham had been involved with the first bronze emissions. During 1874–76 and 1881–82, when the Royal Mint was particularly hard-pressed, the minting of some bronze was again assigned to Heaton's works. These are recognised by the small letter 'H' under the date. The National Insurance Act came into operation in 1911 and generated a heavy demand for silver and bronze coins, and in 1912 Heaton's firm was subcontracted to produce pennies. These have 'H' to the left of the exergue. After the First World War demand for pennies was again high and Heaton minted pennies dated 1918 and 1919. In addition, the firm of Kings Norton Metal Co. Ltd were also called upon to mint pennies, and these were indicated by 'KN'. (20 mm–26 mm.)

Similarities, contrasts, and an odd one out. Before 1902 florins presented a reverse type of the royal arms arranged as four shields (three for 'Widow's Head' emissions). For Edward VII an original design appeared with Britannia standing on the prow of a Roman galley, symbolising British naval might. The first sixpence of 1912 seems identical to that from 1926, though there is one crucial difference: the former contains .925 silver, the latter .500. In 1927 a new type with oak leaves and six acorns emerged, in tandem with the threepence bearing three acorns. Half-crowns presented the royal arms in different manifestations, as shown here with examples from 1885, 1942 and 1962. The odd one out is second from the left: a lead/pewter forgery of a Victorian half-crown. (20 mm–32 mm.)

The first releases, and dates of issue, of Britain's decimal currency with the Queen's effigy designed by Arnold Machin, as on the 1968 'new' five pence. Halfpenny, penny, twopence (1971–1981); five pence, ten pence (1968–1981); fifty pence (1969–1981); twenty pence (1982–1984); one pound (1983–1984). (17 mm–30 mm.)

Tokens, 1850 to 2019

With a full official coinage which included small change emerging in the second third of the nineteenth century, it might be expected that tokens became a thing of the past. This was manifestly not the case. The British public, after several centuries of producing their own unofficial issues, were so wedded to the value of tokens that emissions of them increased across the country to serve in many and diverse contexts, with thousands being issued. Tokens have qualities that standard coinage cannot possess: they can allow for specific practices and customs in precise locations. Other forms of tokens, especially those produced by countermarking, continued to have particular merit, especially during the early part of this period.

A class of token which probably has a heritage beginning in the medieval period was handed out to fruit pickers. A related occupation was that of hop picker, which arose with the introduction of hop cultivation into south-east England from Flanders in the seventeenth century for the brewing of beer (ale, brewed from Anglo-Saxon times, is produced from malt without hops). It was a successful crop and its husbandry spread through Kent and into Sussex. With insufficient local labour to complete its harvest hop pickers were hired from elsewhere, particularly London, and the season became a

Countermarking of regal coinage was causing some annoyance by the 1830s and in 1853 was outlawed, though it did not entirely cease, as evidenced by this 1863 penny, adorned with a crown above 'BC'. Sharp minds quickly realised that the law did not apply to foreign coins and from the late 1860s French five and ten centimes were circulating as small change, mainly in London and the south-east, countermarked with advertising. London's 'Dix Gas Lamp Maker Clerkenwell', 'Pears Soap', and 'Empire Theatre Immense Success' were especially outstanding in this field, the ones here having been applied in the mid-1880s. 'J Hood' may have been James Hood bootmaker or James Hood coffee rooms, or, maybe, John Hood tobacconist – all from London. The practice had waned by the end of the century, though enigmatic pieces continued to be released, as the 1944 farthing with 'S' illustrates. (20 mm–30 mm.)

The large lead token was stamped to represent sixty bushels for Elizabeth Daws at Soggs Farm, Ewhurst, Sussex. The Daws family had been associated with this venture since at least the time of Thomas Daws (b. 1771) and his wife Mary (b. 1786). By around 1850 up to sometime before 1891 their son, another Thomas (b. 1814), ran the farm jointly with his sister Elizabeth (b. 1815). By 1901 it had been passed on to the next Thomas Daws (b. 1848) and his wife Elizabeth (b. 1853). Thus, and giving due regard to its fabric, this token is likely to have been issued from the late 1840s to around 1880 by the Elizabeth born in 1815. At a substantial face value of sixty bushels (480 gallons), it may have been handed to a group of pickers, probably a family, or was exchanged for many tokens, rather like handing over a hundred pennies for a pound coin. William Nash Vinson (1885–1914) moved his hop ground to Hall Place in East Barming, Kent, in 1909 from where he issued this halfpenny token. The following three are fruit pickers' tokens: Hall Marsh Farm, Long Sutton, Lincolnshire, probably *c.* 1900 or later, made from zinc; an aluminium ten shilling piece for W. Thacker, Gedney, also Lincolnshire from around 1930/40; and a slightly later cardboard 'Picker's Ticket' for *6d* from George E. See, 'Fruitgrower', at Four Gotes, Tydd St Giles, Cambridgeshire. (Metal tokens 23 mm–41 mm; cardboard, 58 mm x 50 mm.)

Hop pickers. Posted from Tunbridge Wells, Kent, to Clapham, 4 October 1908, with the message on the reverse reading: 'This is a view of one of the Hop gardens. The picking is all finished now. It has been such a bad year. My holiday is going so quickly. Hope you are well.'

working holiday in the fresh air. They were paid not in cash but in tokens, per bushel picked (eight gallons). In 1931 the rate was 2*d* per bushel. The accumulated tokens would then be redeemed at the end of the season. This helped the farmer's accounting and cash flow, and money did not need to always be on hand. It also discouraged pickers from moving on. A less than official version of this arrangement suggests that the tokens were used as currency within the group of workers on the farm, and to while away the evening gambling at card games.

Tokens used in establishments serving alcohol have an equally long and grey history. Many were issued in the seventeenth century and another spate emerged from around the middle of the nineteenth century. In some areas they were still in use in the 1950s. Philip and Harold Mernick suggest that they were utilised for the prepayment of drinks, thereby preventing the handling of cash by bar staff; supplied by employers to employees for refreshment at approved establishments; to obtain refreshment as part of an entrance fee to a place of entertainment; to avoid laws ruling against cash rewards; and to provide refreshments at meetings held in rented rooms. They were redeemable by the landlord and so were worthless if he left the establishment before doing so, unfortunately for the punters.

W. Morgans issued his 3*d* token for the Cross Hands Hotel, Pontardawe, Glamorgan, dated 1861. A few years later his son John was licensee and countermarked the tokens with his initials, thereby guaranteeing they would be redeemed as before. It was also a cheaper alternative to producing tokens in his name. Isaac Jones (b. 1850) was son of cap maker Happy Jones of Gornal Wood, Dudley. At some date after 1881 Isaac replaced John Greenaway as licensee of Pear Tree Inn. In 1901 his son Eli (b. 1881) was listed as 'Brewer' at his father's pub. Ten years later Eli's mother Mathilda, now a widow, was enumerated as 'Beerhouse Keeper' there, with Eli remaining a brewer. He became licensee of the Pear Tree in 1916, running it until 1930, the period of issue for his token. It was taken over by 'Robinson' who issued this token in *c*. 1938. Sometime before he died Isaac was (also?) running Limerick Inn, from where he issued his token no later than 1910. (21 mm–28 mm.)

Tokens worldwide have been pressed into service in times of war, for both military personnel and civilians. During the First World War tokens were dispensed to combatants on both sides of the conflict incarcerated in prisoner of war camps. As well as being environment-specific, they prohibited the use of a local currency which could have made an escape across country more viable.

In the Second World War areas of Britain were ravaged by bombing raids, leaving many civilians homeless and destitute. So as to ensure that they did not go without a meal the Ministry of Food set up Communal Feeding Centres in vicinities worst affected and by 1943 more than 2,000 were in operation. Various means for payment were in place, such as paper tickets, so in 1942 the ministry instructed that plastic discs be used throughout the nation in what became known as 'British Restaurants'. These tokens were of a larger size for adults, with a smaller version for children, and were colour-coded for specific parts of a meal: tea or coffee, soup, meat, and sweet. Many British Restaurants stayed open for a few years after the end of hostilities.

The beginning of the Co-operative movement can be traced back to the eighteenth century and the changes in society taking place as heavy industries and factories emerged and migration from countryside to urban areas quickened. With difficulties in redeeming tokens issued from 1787, and with a glut of forgeries and the inequity of the truck system, workers began to pool their resources and buy basic household commodities such as bread in bulk. The fundamental concepts underlying this development were

An iron ten centimes token of the BEF (British Expeditionary Force) from the British-run POW camps in France and Belgium during the First World War. From the same conflict, an iron five pfennig of the German-run POW camp in Ohrdruf, Saxe-Coburg-Gotha. On Queen Victoria's marriage to Albert in 1840 Saxe-Coburg-Gotha became the surname of the British royal family. In 1917 George V changed this to 'Windsor'. Two British Restaurant tokens issued during the Second World War for tea (grey) and soup (black) in Rhyl. (18 mm–31 mm.) (British Restaurant tokens courtesy of Philip and Harold Mernick)

increasingly discussed in the early decades of the nineteenth century and by 1844 the first successful society, the 'Rochdale Society of Equitable Pioneers', opened its shop for two evenings a week. Over the ensuing decades other societies were created which followed the principles laid down in Rochdale, and slowly the range of goods available in their shops increased.

Cheaply produced metallic tokens were probably introduced in the mid-1850s, though other materials such as plastic and crushed fibre were exploited, and comprised a range of denominations, often of different shapes or colours. Of the three main categories of token, the first were handed out as dividend checks to members for the value of each purchase and redeemed on Dividend-day, which was usually half-yearly. If the dividend was 10 per cent (it could vary) then for every £10 in checks a cash payment of £1 would be given. Unfortunately this system could be abused and undermined: forgeries of high-value checks appeared; better-off members could buy tokens in the possession of the less affluent, probably taking advantage of someone's situation; and the better-off might also hold on to their tokens in the hope that dividends would be higher in the future. A second type of token issued by Co-operative Societies were those for the prepayment of certain items – bread, milk, and coal in particular. This scheme benefited all concerned; for example, a usual week's supply of these consumables would be known and on payday tokens for this amount bought at the local shop, thus ensuring that whatever financial crisis might intervene for the rest of the week these commodities would be accessible. The specifications used for bread were not consistent across the country and were determined by each society's methods of working: it could be sold by

Four dividend checks: Gwynfi, Manchester & Salford and Guide Post (manufactured in bronze as suits its higher value). Bread tokens: Northampton, Royal Arsenal, Cowes, Wellingborough, Chard and Frome. Milk tokens: Pontycymmer, Long Buckley and Barry. (19 mm–31 mm.)

Old habits continue: two modern supermarket trolley tokens. They are of value in a specific context as substitutes for coins of the realm and may be used for advertising purposes. (22 mm.)

size, cost, or by weight, including the now obsolete quartern loaf – one which weighed 4 pounds. The advantage of these tokens for, say, the milkman, is that money did not have to change hands, deliveries were speeded up and the amount required by each household would be represented in the number of tokens left out. The third type were mutuality tokens, which were given to members seeking a loan. Rather than hand out cash (which might be spent on other articles or services elsewhere), the tokens could only be spent in the relevant dry goods section of the Co-op.

Some of these tokens (and others) will be remembered by older readers. However, the role of tokens in the story of small change does not end in the past. They have been of crucial worth and practical value for centuries: they are also with us today in many and varied contexts. Their pedigree is impressive.

Acknowledgements

With due admission that they are not responsible for any errors in *Small Change*, special recognition is deserved by:

Allan Cawley

Charles Eaves at *All Our Yesterdays*, Colwyn Bay, at http://yesterdaytoday.co/

Mostafa Faghfoury, *Cyrus Coins*, Canada, at https://www.vcoins.com/en/stores/cyrus_coins-28/ancient-coins/Default.aspx?

Valerie Hailwood

Adrian Hughes, Home Front Museum, Llandudno, at http://homefrontmuseum.co.uk

Barry Jones

Nick Jowett and the *Great Orme Bronze Age Mines*, at https://www.greatermemines.info

Dane Kurth at www.wildwinds.com. 'The WildWinds website has been created as a reference and attribution resource in the field of ancient numismatics.'

Philip and Harold Mernick at http://www.mernick.org.uk. 'We have many collecting interests. Online content has been created for some of these, with the aim of passing on our information to anyone else with similar interests.'

Chris Rudd and Liz Cottam, *Chris Rudd Ltd*, at www.celticcoins.com. 'Dedicated exclusively to Celtic coins'.

Museums Victoria, Melbourne, Australia, at https://collections.museumvictoria.com.au/ 'Museums Victoria supports and encourages public access to our collection by offering image downloads for reuse.'

Additionally, a massive thanks goes out to all those who lent coins or supplied images of items from their collections, and who wish to remain anonymous.

About the Author

Peter has a background in academic research and was a part-time university lecturer. He is a Fellow of the Royal Numismatic Society and has published a number of papers in this field. He recently gained the Advanced Diploma in Local History at the University of Oxford. In addition, he has been a keen writer of fiction for many years, winning a number of competitions.